DOCTORS' WIVES

DOCTORS' WIVES

The Truth About Medical Marriages

Cynthia S. Smith

SEAVIEW BOOKS / NEW YORK

From pp. 43, 75, 88 (approximately 400 words) in BRAIN SURGEON by Lawrence Shainberg (J. B. Lippincott Company). Copyright © 1979 by Lawrence Shainberg. Reprinted by permission of Harper & Row, Publishers, Inc.

Manufactured in the United States of America.

FIRST EDITION

Library of Congress Cataloging in Publication Data

Smith, Cynthia S
    Doctors' wives.

    Bibliography: p.
       1. Physicians' wives. 2. Physicians' wives—United States. I. Title.
R707.2.S63   306.8'7'08861   80-52419
ISBN 0-87223-650-1

Designed by M. Franklin-Plympton

Note to the Reader

The case histories in this book are based on real people and are the result of extensive research and interviews. Names and some personal details have been altered to protect the privacy of those involved.

To David, Hillary, and Sarah, the three
people who make me possible.

Acknowledgments

To Julian Perlman, whose faith and friendship helped give life to the project. To Robert Nevin, whose support and encouragement helped it grow.

Contents

DOCTORS' WIVES

INTRODUCTION

The Myth Versus the Reality of Medical Marriages

Marry a doctor and you've got it all. The societal stamp of success. Wealth, prestige, the approval of your family, and the envy of your peers. What more could any woman want?

For starters, how about companionship, loving attention, family life, a full-time husband? Is that asking too much of a marriage? If your husband is a man of medicine who deals daily in life and death and must respond first to more vital needs than your emotional well-being, it is.

We on the outside tend to regard doctors' wives as a pampered spoiled lot who lead lives of smug security married to those powerful, romantic heroes in white who hold the secrets to our mortality. That's the view from the outside. But the inside facts are very different. We all enter situations with certain expectations—some realistic, some romantic. Marriage is one of those areas where we tend to lean more heavily toward the romantic at the outset, and happiness can only be achieved by reconciliations with the realistic.

One problem with marrying a doctor is that no amount

of awareness can prepare a woman for the feelings of abandonment and rejection she experiences. When that omnipresent beeper goes off to summon him away from her side to answer someone else's call . . . when she has to tell the children that Daddy can't come to graduation because he must be with a patient—it takes a superwoman to smile and not feel that if he really loved her, he could somehow make other arrangements to accommodate *her* needs. And how can she handle that insidious niggling suspicion that his dedication to medicine is based on his craving for ego fulfillment rather than nobler motivations?

The severe penalties exacted upon the souls and psyches of women who marry physicians have become apparent over the past few years during my tenure as editor and publisher of *Medical/Mrs.*, the magazine for doctors' wives. Our first issue contained an article by the wife of a world-famous neurosurgeon. It exposed a shocking picture of private disappointments, now being made public, of the pain, frustration, and often sheer misery of being a doctor's wife. The response to this article was staggering. The tone and quantity of the mail suggested a pervasive undercurrent of disillusionment among these women that belied the conventional picture of the fortunate, successfully married queen-bee-of-the-community who has it made.

To bring these feelings out into the open, to see if in fact they existed, *Medical/Mrs.* created a research study questionnaire entitled "A Doctor's Wife: The Myth vs. the Reality" (reprinted below) and inserted it into the magazine.

The response was overwhelming. What emerged was a picture of women whose prenuptial conceptions of marriage were very little like the reality they eventually found. Before marriage, 67.6 percent felt they had achieved every woman's dream when they married doctors. Yet 51.7 percent reported that they were disappointed in their expecta-

A Doctor's Wife: The Myth vs. the Reality

Let's explode the "doctor's wife" myth . . . Give us YOUR opinion!

Marry a doctor and you have achieved the societal stamp of success . . . the fulfillment of the female dream. But is it actually what you expected and what society promised?

MEDICAL/MRS. is doing a research study to evaluate how the role of doctor's wife today reconciles with her expectations. We would appreciate your input. If you wish to remain anonymous, you needn't sign your name. If you choose to identify yourself, be assured that no confidences will be violated and no quotes attributed unless specifically authorized.

BEFORE MARRIAGE

1. Did you have specific thoughts about marrying a doctor? ___yes ___no
2. Was it a positive picture? ___yes ___no
3. If positive, was this reinforced by ___the media? ___family?
4. Did the image of doctor's wife convey ___prestige? ___security? ___happiness? ___pride?
5. Did a doctor present a romantic heroic image to you? ___yes ___no
6. Did the fact that your future husband was to be a doctor affect your attitude toward him favorably? ___yes ___no
7. Did you envision yourself a helpmeet to a man of service? ___yes ___no
8. Honestly, did you feel you had made a "good marriage"—achieved the everywoman's dream—when you married a doctor? ___yes ___no

AFTER MARRIAGE

9. How many years have you been married? ___
10. Did you help put him through medical school? ___yes ___no
11. Have you been disappointed in any of your expectations? ___yes ___no
12. If "yes," in approximately what year of your marriage did you become aware of your feelings? ___
13. Do you feel deprived of companionship in your marriage? ___yes ___no
14. Do you often feel lonely? ___yes ___no
15. Do you resent your husband's absences and work demands? ___never ___sometimes ___often
16. Do you feel your husband's profession imposes an unfair burden on you? ___yes ___no
    On your children? ___yes ___no
17. Have you been forced to make many emotional compromises in your marriage? ___yes ___no
18. Do you believe your husband has made any for you? ___yes ___no
19. Do you suffer due to the "God" status your husband enjoys? ___yes ___no
20. Did you realistically anticipate the difficulties in being a doctor's wife? ___yes ___no
21. Were your "before marriage" expectations met? ___yes ___no
22. Do you enjoy being a doctor's wife? ___yes ___no
23. If you had it to do again, would you marry a doctor? ___yes ___no
24. Would you encourage your daughter to marry one? ___yes ___no

tions; 64 percent felt *they* had to make the "emotional compromises."

Do they suffer due to the "God" status their husbands enjoy? Nearly half, 48.2 percent, said, emphatically, "Yes."

As one woman married to a doctor for twenty-four years told us: "I find we keep our hurts to ourselves and it certainly helps to know that others have the same feelings and needs. I often think that it's just me, but I'm beginning to think there are hundreds out there just like *me!*"

Apparently we had touched a wellspring of sublimated pain that desperately needed an outlet. But when you think about it, what's so surprising? One of the frustrations a doctor's wife suffers is the inability to get anyone to take her complaints seriously. After all, it's a little awkward to discuss the deficiencies of her domestic life when she's talking on her Princess phone from the den of her $200,000 home. Not only is it embarrassing, but she is blocked by her own guilt. How can she in good conscience be unhappy when she has achieved the female American dream—she is a DOCTOR'S WIFE!

What we learned is that despite the great publicity, and the presumed perfect existence, marriage to a doctor is no bed of roses. True, there are many medical wives who adore the perks and prestige, for example, Mrs. S. C. from New York City, who wrote, "Who cares about a successful marriage as long as you get to drive your Lincoln to the club every day?" And of course, not all doctors are failures as husbands. However, medicine does tend to attract a type of driven, uncompromising individual to start with . . . and the intense demands of the profession plus the adulation heaped upon its practitioners serve to mold them into men who are unsatisfactory partners in life. So what happens to the women who enter marriages with doctors and are not prepared for the emotional disappointments? What causes the failure of the female American dream?

1

The Bride's Pride . . .
She Married a Doctor!

"Meet my son-in-law the doctor." Oh, what smug satisfaction and pride are packed into those words. Our daughter has proven her worthiness and therefore ours . . . she has reached the pinnacle of marital success by bringing a young god into the family. She will most assuredly be rich and respected, envied and admired. She (and we) must have done something right to have captured so superior a prize. That she has succeeded in attracting such a star proves her value beyond a doubt, because isn't that the touchstone by which young women have always been measured?

Only in recent years, thanks to awareness stimulated by the women's movement, has there been any drive to rate women by their own achievements rather than those of their spouses. Even today, with women moving into law, medicine, and executive suites, the tendency is still to judge females by their abilities to snare worthy spouses rather than by their abilities to succeed in worthy careers.

On the marital evaluation scale, a doctor rates extremely high. In the folklore of Jewish mothers, it has always been an accepted fact that marrying off a daughter to a doctor is the epitome of social achievement. There were no lengths to which a mother would not go to accomplish this enviable feat. There is a story of a woman seated in the dining room in Grossinger's, the renowned hostelry in the Catskill Mountains of New York, who suddenly arose in the middle of dinner one evening, groaning loudly, "Oh, oh—is there a doctor in the house?" Within minutes, a young man rushed to her side. "Can I help you, madam?" he asked solicitously, in his best professional manner. She beamed at him and pointed proudly to the young woman seated next to her. "Yes, doctor, meet my daughter, Rosalie!"

The reasons for a doctor's superior standing in the marriage market are myriad, but perhaps the most important is status. For medicine is the one profession in the world that transcends all class considerations. The yardstick for social status is calibrated according to power—not money, not family, not achievement, not fame, but the power that these advantages confer. Then who has greater power than a doctor—for isn't he the only one who can exercise any effect on the life and death of everyone?

Millionaires and movie stars, tycoons and tyrants, may buy or control people, but they are powerless when it comes to controlling their own bodies. There is an inverse ratio between power and dependency: the stronger and more powerful you become, the less need you have for others. Of course, there are qualitative differences to needs. An international shipping tycoon may need his accountant and lawyer. But his life doesn't hang on that dependency. And chances are he has some knowledge and expertise in those areas so that the accountant and lawyer actually rely heavily on his input and approval. However, when it comes to health, he is totally at the mercy of the medical profession. He may have closed a deal on Monday to take over all of OPEC's oil fields, a deal which would make him the most famous, powerful person in the world, answerable to virtually no one. But if on Tuesday he discovers he has a brain tumor, the great man is suddenly reduced to total dependency on a neurosurgeon.

Doctors are totally cognizant of their power, and they revel in it. A famous brain surgeon stated blatantly that power is the ultimate motivation for most neurosurgeons. As the fictitiously named, but real, "Dr. Brockman" put it in the book *Brain Surgeon*, "What was surgery after all but an ultimate expression of technology? And what was technology but an expression of the need to manage power?" Doctors are arrogantly, almost savagely, aware of their uniquely omnipotent positions.

And let's not forget the media hype toward building the image of those noble, romantic men of healing. Literature, movies, and television abound in medical heroes. There has never been a TV season without at least one major doctor series at the top of the ratings . . . from Drs. Kildare, Marcus Welby, and Hawkeye Pierce to the ever-popular soap operas *As the World Turns*, *General Hospital*, *One Life to Live*, *The Doctors*. Millions of people tune in daily to watch the activities and interactions of those dashing, dedicated men in white. Although after watching a few episodes you wonder how the good doctors can cope with curing since so much of their energies seem to be devoted to soul-racking emotional and sexual conflicts.

The fascination with fictional doctors goes further than just mere curiosity; it caters to a deep desire in all of us to have an omniscient human panacea for all our bodily ills . . . a caring, skillful, infallible being who can guarantee solutions. Since medicine, despite its advances, is still an inexact science, that wish continues to remain one of wistful unfulfillment for most of us. But others handle it differently by merging fantasy with fact and look upon these TV doctors as actual physicians. The TV actor Don

Hastings, who plays Dr. Bob Hughes on the soap opera *As the World Turns*, was actually invited by the mayor of a small Midwest town that had lost its physician to take over the practice! Jim Pritchett, who plays Matt Powers on *The Doctors*, is frequently asked by strangers for professional medical advice. Henderson Forsythe, who also appears in *As the World Turns*, recalls a woman stopped him on the street to chat and then introduced him to her husband: "Dear, this is Dr. Stewart." Most of their fan letters come from hospitalized patients.

There is a mystique about medicine and the men who practice it that fascinates us all. It evolves from an olio of feelings like fear of dying, concerns about our health, and the abysmal ignorance most of us have of the details and functioning of our physical machinery. It is unavoidable to feel a certain amount of admiration for anyone who has seen, handled, and has a working familiarity with our insides, especially today with the incredible advances in surgery where hearts and arteries are restructured and severed extremities are reattached. It is almost wondrous to be chatting over coffee with a surgeon who has just completed a triple heart bypass and thereby conceivably extended the life of a previously doomed individual. Even a cynical sophisticate may find it hard to regard the surgeon with anything but awe. Imagine the bedazzlement of a young woman in a starry-eyed prenuptial state who dreams of a glowing future spent as the partner of this near-god figure.

This attitude was manifest in the results of the *Medical/ Mrs.* research study questionnaire "A Doctor's Wife: The Myth vs. the Reality." In answer to the "before marriage" question: "Did a doctor present a romantic, heroic image to you?" 45 percent said "Yes." "Did you envision yourself a helpmeet to a man of service?" A whopping 70 percent answered in the affirmative. And the prestige factor weighed heavily in the premarital considerations. "Did the image of a doctor's wife convey prestige?" Fifty-seven percent said "Yes."

The title "doctor" is one that carries instant entrée and respect anywhere, at all social and economic levels. When you are Mrs. Doctor, you ride right to the top with him. Pretty heady stuff.

And let's not overlook that other pleasant peripheral benefit of the medical marriage—money and security. In the *Medical/Mrs.* research study, to the question "Did the image of a doctor's wife convey security?" 54 percent said "Yes."

Doctors as a group command one of the highest median incomes in the nation—$75,000 per year. And that's just a median. Even young residents who used to struggle along on $50 a month now start with the highly respectable salary of $20,000 a year. A young woman marrying a doctor can look forward to the comfortable assurance of a life of affluence . . . to the great luxury of living with a man whose job security is never threatened.

As Phil Donahue, host of the popular talk show, mentioned to an audience of AMA Auxiliary wives when the subject of the day was the life of a doctor's wife, "Your husband can never get fired." He pointed out that most people work at the whim of others, often one individual. Some neurotic superior could look into his shaving mirror one morning and capriciously decide "Harry has to go"— and that's the end of poor Harry. Which means Harry's wife lives with a man who dwells with daily dread for his job security, which has to affect the family's quality of life. But a doctor can never lose his job and therefore doesn't live with the sort of economic uncertainties that other mortals endure. True, he can lose a patient or two, or even a hospital affiliation—but never his livelihood. The moment he gets that M.D. degree, his successful economic future is absolute and secure.

What more could a woman want of a marriage? Prestige,

security, wealth, the companionship of a man who is revered
and respected . . . even that usually elusive but eternally
coveted prize—parental approval.

When the final "before marriage" question was asked:
"Honestly, did you feel you had made a 'good marriage'—
achieved every woman's dream—when you married a doctor?" 67.6 percent said "Yes!"

Well done, young woman. You've married a doctor. Your
future is made. Or is it?

II

The Beginning: Medical School Marriages and the P.H.T. Degree (Putting Hubby Through)

During the four years Tom was in medical school, Joan worked as a secretary, waitress, and at any other jobs she could pick up to support them through those lean years. It was difficult for her, but Joan felt the drudgery was temporary and looked forward to an easy, secure life when Tom went into private practice. Ten years later, Tom divorced Joan to marry his office nurse. The story is a familiar one. One out of six medical school marriages self-destruct within ten years of graduation. The intensive isolation of those years of schooling, the wife's unrealistic expectations of an idyllic future, the changes that take place in a young man as he undergoes medical education, all these factors subject medical school marriages to stresses that not all can survive.

Joan had been a freshman in college when she met Tom,

who was then a senior, and they married the following year. When Tom entered medical school, Joan quit college and gave up her own career plans in order to support them. Without a college degree, Joan could not get a high-level job, and the salary she earned as a secretary made living tight. She marketed carefully on the way home each evening, came home to their cramped apartment, and cooked and served dinner. Then Tom went into the small bedroom and closed the door to study while she cleaned the dishes, the house, did the laundry and ironing, and then fell asleep exhausted in front of the TV. Since weekends were little different, with Tom studying constantly, Joan augmented their income by working as a waitress in a local restaurant.

The pressure of the two jobs, wage earner and homemaker, was burden enough. But the worst part was the loneliness—the lack of companionship, relationship, and affection. Joan managed to sustain her spirits through it all by telling herself this hellish existence was just a passing period, an investment that would ultimately produce a life of pleasure, ease, and total happiness. Besides, soon school would be over and then internship would surely be easier.

After graduation, Tom found an internship in a hospital in another city and they pulled up roots to move to a strange community where Joan knew absolutely no one. The financial load was easier because Tom was now earning an income, but the loneliness became intolerable. Instead of seeing more of Tom, as she had anticipated, she now saw less. At least in medical school, he was home, albeit closeted in another room. But there was the comfort of the physical presence of another human being. Now he was rarely home, and when he was it was only only to fall into an exhausted sleep.

Tom's real life and world seemed to be the hospital, and Joan sensed herself an outsider. When they did get a chance to talk, it was only to hear about people she did not know, about activities with which she had no familiarity.

"When he gets into private practice and we have a home and life together, then things will be better," Joan comforted herself. But two years after Tom started in private practice, ten years after they were married, Tom left the woman who by now had become an uninteresting stranger to him to start a fresh alliance with his young office nurse who shared his new life completely.

Was Tom a cad or just a person caught in a very complex human situation? For starters, consider the cast of characters in this story. Here we have an ambitious young man who has driven himself in college to achieve grades that will gain him admission to medical school. Competition being what it is for the few places that exist in U.S. medical schools, the fortunate few who make it have paid a heavy toll of deprivation of social life, sex life, and all the elements that go into the development and maturation of a solid, well-adjusted human being.

Since he has had little chance to make contact with many young women in college, and thus amassed only very minimal experience in learning how to handle himself in social interaction, his ineptitude and inadequacy lead him to tie up with the first young woman who would have him. And to marry her.

In a study made by *Medical Opinion* magazine in June 1973, three-fourths of doctors at that time aged over fifty had married before completion of their formal training. The specialties varied in their marital patterns. GPs were most likely to marry prior to completion of medical school and surgeons least likely. More than half of those who become family practitioners were married before getting out of medical school. Almost the same percentage of surgeons were single up to that point, then married during internship and residency.

Envision the young premed student who is obsessed with the knowledge that he must achieve superlative grades if he wishes to stand a chance of making it in his chosen career. It has been drummed into his head that nothing less than a 3.8 average will earn consideration for even an interview for an opening at any accredited medical school. He has heard the dreadful stories of students who applied to twenty-five medical schools and received twenty-five rejections. He has read the newspaper articles about young people going to Italy, Mexico, and wherever in order to get a medical education that had been denied to them here. The competition for marks in premed days is fierce and fanatic, and time off for relaxation and socializing is a luxury that cannot be even considered. Constant work and poring over books is the only route to follow. Studies made in the sixties and seventies report that most medical students are obsessive-compulsive personalities—hardworking, precise, and controlled. They would have to be in order to succeed in that madly competitive arena.

But because the young man has a strong career drive does not mean that he has a weak sex drive. The desires for pleasures of the flesh are there—it's just the time that isn't. He longs for female companionship and sexual partnership, but does not have the social aptitude, finesse, and time to develop relationships. As one student tells it: "A lot of unmarried students practice abstinence because there's just no time. You can't devote all the time and effort to taking a date out, getting to know her, for just that one instant [of sex]. Therefore I think a lot of single students lean toward masturbation." It follows that the easiest way to handle the whole problem is to marry and thus be assured of total fulfillment of all social and sexual needs in one handy package.

Now we come to the marital relationship. This is a young man who has spent his adult life with one goal, one mission—to succeed in his career. He has not learned about human considerations that evolve in a relationship, about the give-and-take required to effect a successful marriage. He has developed no antenna to anyone's sensitivities other than his own. It's a serious defect that exacts a damaging toll on young medical school marriages, as shown in this letter from a young woman who had been living with a doctor for a year and a half.

Having been with a doctor now for a year and a half, I have come to many actualizations about the medical profession. Do doctors really make lousy husbands? Are they really that bad a risk? The fact that these people experience life and death every day is, to me, no excuse for their being rather emotionally retarded and unwilling to cope with their *real* feelings. It's as if there is no room, or it's too threatening. What a shameful denial of pleasure that perhaps could teach them to find more meaning and understanding of themselves and of their work!

I agree that priorities must be clearly established at home; work is a given and the demands on medicine are pronounced. But there must be some working with the personal in the relationship. Forget discussions on whose life is more important, but get into the humanity of living, and consciously set time aside to be together. This is the survival kit of any marriage. And where do doctors get off with having it any other way? They wouldn't treat their practices, patients, hospital relationships like that. Running a marriage is like running a business or a practice. Women clearly have to be aware of the demands medicine places on their men. But doctors, as men relating to their women, must realize their responsibilities as partners. Do you think doctors sabotage their relationships/marriages because they can't deal with the personal aspects of life, and find feelings and emotions too threatening after all those years of studying to be the people-considered-nearest-to-gods? Is it too much of an ego deflation to come home and only be just plain Joe Schmedley?

How can it be better constructed so that for all the years it takes to train someone to be a doctor, *along the way he*

*also experiences training to be an emotionally healthy, up-
front, here and now, feeling individual?* Truly, doctors'
emotional development is asked to take a back seat whilst
they bury their noses in text books for the next 14 years of
their lives. I was startled to learn that, while for the past
13 years, I've been coming together psychologically, living
in our times (coming out in the 60s, refining that learning
experience and bringing it through the eye of the needle in
the 70s, hoofing it from one coast to another), Tom has
literally had his nose in books and is *now* just beginning
to realize what else is out there in the real world. He's
having to learn to deal with his very most personal feelings
(which is a classic "passages" since he's going through the
30th gate in March), and he doesn't have much experience
to really cope, except in an academic way.

The reality of life with such a man is a shock to a young
wife, especially one who has entered the marriage with the
exalted expectations created by peer envy and parental approval. Instead of an idyllic existence with a prince, she finds
herself locked in with a companion who never accompanies
her, a home-sharer who gives no share of himself, a human
being who extends little humanistic understanding to her.
She is virtually alone, but worse; not only has she lost her
freedom, but she finds she now has the responsibility of
caring for his needs as well as her own. It's a bind that leaves
her angry, resentful, and guilty.

Now what's been happening to him through all this
travail? What sort of changes are taking place within this
controlled psyche now that he has finally reached his goal?

Let's start with the shock of the beginning—the fateful
freshman fall when he enters medical school. Here's a young
man who has just spent the summer on a glorious cloud,
basking in the approval, admiration, and envy of family
and friends. As the culmination of years of dedicated hard
work, he has achieved the impossible dream—admission
to medical school. All his life he has been a superb student,

and if there is one thing he's sure of it is his ability to excel with ease in any academic situation. He enters medical school in the fall, proud, assured, one of the chosen few.

Now comes the horribly rude awakening. In medical school *everyone* is a hotshot . . . every student has been a superachiever or he wouldn't be there. Suddenly our young man is faced with the unfamiliar position of being just an average student, one of many. He's no longer a star. Competition among this group is a different ball game than among the run-of-the-norm kids in high school or even among the students in college who were equally intelligent but far less motivated than he.

This sudden drop in status constitutes a very large blow indeed. Throughout school, his sense of self-value has been almost solely supported by that super scholastic superiority. He never made it in the jock world, was pretty much a bust in the social scene. But one area in which he was a sure standout was in academia.

Suddenly he must accept the fact that his one claim to fame is gone. It's shocking, sobering, and very humbling.

"For many entering freshmen, medical school represents a first experience in being a 'second-class citizen,' not only in terms of faculty and hospital staff but also in terms of their peers. For students accustomed to being unquestionably at the top of the academic heap, often without much effort, confrontation with students of superior ability can be a shattering experience. Objectively, most freshmen are fully aware that they are outstanding; national statistics bear out that students accepted into medical school are high achievers—intelligent, able and strongly motivated. Yet objective awareness conflicts with the shocking experience of many entering students. 'You find you're no longer at the top of the pile, the *it*. You are confronted by others twice as smart as you.' "

Not only that—it's downright frightening. Suddenly a new experience enters his academic life—fear . . . fear that

he may not be able to make it. Fear of not being able to do
the work is a major source of stress for first-year students.
"When I came here, I'd never had an F in my life. On my
first exam I panicked and I failed." Fear and the actual experience of failure obviously engender self-doubts, which in
turn affect the student's ability to perform. "I was top of
my class in high school, and in college I graduated summa
cum laude. In the middle of my first semester here, I was
barely passing. Is med school too big for me to handle? Am
I smart enough?" "The first semester I was scared to death
all the time. It was the most depressing three months of
my life. I had periods when I was so paralyzed with fear I
couldn't study."

This popular medical school litany illustrates how the fear
persists throughout the training years.

PREMED STUDENT: "Am I going to get in?"

FRESHMAN: "Will I make it?"

SOPHOMORE: "Do I really want to do this?"

JUNIOR: "Will I ever know enough?"

SENIOR: "Will I ever know enough?"

INTERN: "Will I ever know enough?"

RESIDENT: "Will I ever know enough?"

The situation is not helped by unsympathetic medical
school faculties who seem to enjoy treating first-year students as infantile cretins. Especially the Ph.D. scientists who
resent teaching and regard it as an infringement on time
that would be better spent in their own research. Unfortunately, a good part of first- and second-year medical
school involves medically oriented but nonclinical subjects
such as biochemistry, genetics, microbiology, physiology,
histology, neuroanatomy. And the instructors teach the same
courses to science graduate students who intend to spend
their lives in such work and are thus more respected by
the faculty. So the neophyte medic finds himself in another
unfamiliar stressful situation—that of a student with least-
favored status who is regarded with condescension by his

teachers. It's tough to take—especially after his golden-boy academic history.

And then there's that other basic apprehension that has been gnawing at his gut for years. All this time, he's been working to get into med school in order to become a doctor. OK, he's in—he has proven to himself beyond a doubt that he is a good student. Now he must face up to the question that's been buried in his innards all these years: will he be a good doctor?

There are God-given abilities in medicine as in any other field. The talent for surgery requires a confluence of dexterity ("golden hands"), instinctual judgment, cool ability to make instant decisions and act fast. To be an outstanding diagnostician calls for a superb memory, the ability to logically relate elements, a sort of Sherlock Holmesian deductive-reasoning genius. There are a myriad of specialized areas in medicine, and there are plenty of people who have the special aptitudes needed to rise to the top of the heap in those fields.

Will our young man be one of the biggies? Does he have that special gift that will make him a star among stars? Or will he end up just an average, competent practitioner?

Now is the time he will find out. Now is the moment he pits himself against his medical peers and finds out how he will rate in life.

It's sobering and nerve-racking. And these rather naïve unworldly young men, who have dwelled in ivory tower isolation for all their lives, are often unprepared and unable to cope with unpleasant realities and sometimes stunning setbacks to their egos. They often resort to crutches and easy outs, such as drugs and alcohol. Twenty-three percent of medical students have used amphetamines more than once and 15 percent continue to use them after their clinical years begin. And for some, the situation becomes impossible to handle. At representative medical schools between 20 and 30 percent of the students seek assistance from staff psychiatrists, and many seek help outside lest their fears of inadequacy become part of their official records. Suicide is the highest cause of death among medical students. The adjustment to medical school takes a terrible toll on the soul.

So you have a young man who comes home from school each day beaten down by the day's assaults, unsure, angry, puzzled. What he really needs to find when he crosses the home threshold is a refuge and a sympathetic mother who believes in him implicitly, shores up his battered psyche, gives him his slippers and a good dinner, and tiptoes around the house to avoid disturbing sonny boy while he studies.

Instead, he finds a seething young wife who is exhausted from her day's work, weary of her double burden, a troubled being who wants to talk out her own fears, questions, and problems—who becomes resentful when he shuts that door on her every night. His total lack of experience with women, his inability to relate to emotional needs of others, serves him very poorly and he is helpless to deal with the eruptions occurring in their marriage.

If she can get him to see her side and they work out their difficulties either alone or with help, the marriage has a chance. But if, as so often occurs, his method of coping with what he considers her unreasonable demands is a continuation of his closed-door policy, then she must compromise or quit. And that starts seeds of difficulties that grow as the years go on. Resentment, besides being one of the most destructive emotions because it blames someone else for your troubles, is also often a hidden emotion. You can keep it bottled up inside of you, slowly letting it fester instead of dealing with the problem.

Unfortunately, compromise, which is the basis of a marital relationship, is an activity that comes hard to men of medicine. In the *Medical/Mrs.* research study, the question "Have you been forced to make many emotional compromises in your marriage?" elicited a 64 percent "Yes" response. As to "Do you believe your husband has made any for you?" only 45 percent thought he had.

A prerequisite to compromise is the acceptance of one's potential fallibility. "I could be wrong and you could be right" is the beginning of the granting of concessions that lead to compromise. But a doctor admitting he could be in error? The rigidity of the medical personality makes that sort of situation a rarity indeed. At a dinner party table one evening, a prominent surgeon was chided by one of the guests for his and other doctors' godlike assurance. His reaction came out in tight-lipped fury: "I'd be a damned lousy surgeon if I wasn't sure I was right before I cut into a patient." And there is truth to that. Because quick judgments and instant decision-making are vital to medical performance. A vacillating doctor can mean death for a patient whose case demands quick action. Does this uncompromising assurance develop in a doctor's career, or does the field attract the sort of individual to whom the self-righteous posture is natural?

Neither husbands nor wives emerge from the medical school years the same people they were when, filled with dreams, they began.

A published profile (*CIBA Journal*/Dec. 1, 1973) portrays the entering medical student as humanistically inclined and relatively uncritical. He wants to help people and seeks the further specialized training necessary to achieve his altruistic goal. He expects to find in medical school a world where his humanistic values are shared.

Instead, he finds school a place of tension, pressure, and competition. He finds, as he would in any school, professors who are hard to please, lectures and courses that are poorly organized and repetitious, and a segmented curriculum that seems to bear little relationship to caring for people. The excitement of new experiences, whether it's the first approach to a cadaver or a real patient, is overshadowed by the sense of inadequacy the student feels. House staff, faculty, other students, sometimes even secretaries, seem to know more than he can ever hope to learn.

A wife whose marriage survived recalls that her husband's isolation from the world was one of the hardest things for her to understand. "Medicine," she said, "is an all-consuming world. We all know that. But it's an abrupt change in medical school. He used to read, watch TV, keep up with things. But suddenly he didn't care if there was a threat of war or a gas shortage or some other national crisis. His thoughts were all on fluids and electrolytes and anatomical dissections." Others have called medical school a cloistered existence where intellectual demands are all that matters, and emotional needs, both of the student and his family, are allowed to slide.

The fantasy of a carefree and happy medical student is then no more than a fantasy. The profile cited earlier claims that by the middle of the fourth year the student has become an insensitive human computer, hard to approach, cynical, scientifically rather than humanistically oriented. Of course, some students escape these disastrous effects almost completely; others, by graduation, regain most of their earlier humanitarian attitudes. For some, the change is permanent; for all, there is some degree of change.

"She just didn't grow with him" is the standard pat comment often heard by way of explanation for doctors' divorces. "But how," wailed one ex-wife, "could I grow with him when he was never around?"

Too often, the survival method adopted by unhappy medical school wives is to delude themselves into expecting that everything will fall into place magically after graduation.

To quote a surgeon's wife: "When you let the fantasy speak for you, it says 'after medical school it will be better; after the residency it will be better; after he passes the boards . . .' "

Confessed one ex-wife: "I used to dream about his first

year in practice. It was all I could think about, all that kept me going."

This sort of dreaming leads to those infamous P.H.T. degree (Putting Hubby Through), where the wife sacrifices the present for the rosy expectation of being rewarded in the future.

It rarely happens that way. And such a head-in-the-sand approach to the problem prevents her from facing the facts as they are and reconciling herself to taking steps that will really resolve the situation—for now and always.

When the question "What causes those medical school marriages to falter . . . and can they be saved?" was posed to Dr. Myra Hatterer, a psychiatrist affiliated with Columbia University College of Physicians and Surgeons in New York City, her response was:

> Marriage, be it medical or any other, is a sharing situation. When he is in medical school, and afterwards when he is a house officer and then in private practice, neither husband nor wife is prepared for the tremendous demands on his time and emotions. If the marriage is basically a good one, they can work it out together. If the wife's expectations are not met, she will, of course, be resentful. If the marriage is important to him, he has to make time to incorporate her into his life in some way and to recognize her needs. Today, with the advent of group practices and other arrangements, a doctor does not have to work 120 hours a week. But if he is the kind who wants this sort of work schedule, if he is intent on career building or on an ego trip that needs gratification, then there is no room for her, and she had better be prepared. There is responsibility on both sides to work out the demands of his work and her needs.

Judith Alter, director of public information at the Texas College of Osteopathic Medicine and herself the wife of a doctor, believes that being forewarned is being forearmed. When she speaks to groups of wives of entering students, she begins her presentation with the suggestion that they look at the faces around them. "One out of every six of you will be divorced within ten years."

Unfortunately, Ms. Alter has found that the young wives rarely believe her. The usual attitude is "Maybe you, but not me." Statistically, however, it will happen—and within ten years.

Why the hiatus period? Why do the preponderance of medical school marriages break up those many years later? Why does the breakup not happen immediately while the travail is in progress?

From her vantage point: She hangs on in the hope that things will change for the better once he is happily and securely settled into a practice and family life. So she swallows her sadness and buries her angers—and waits for the golden age.

From his vantage point: He's too busy and involved in medicine to be seriously concerned with marital problems, which he looks upon as her hang-ups. Even if her discontent has been expressed aggressively and offensively, he still needs her services and has no time or confidence to seek a replacement—yet. But once the doctor-deification process begins, once he hits those hospital floors in his godlike role and starts to see himself as a desirable, dashing figure reflected in the eyes of patients and nurses, then he's ripe and ready for a change.

III

The Deification of the Doctor: How Do You Live with God?

"Doctor—how is my husband today?" The elderly woman's face as she confronts intern Joe Dasher outside her husband's room in the hospital corridor is a ravaged mixture of fear, exhaustion, and despair. Her future hangs on the young doctor's words, and the deference in her tone reveals her total dependency on the talents and abilities of this twenty-six-year-old physician.

"He's much better, Mrs. Roberts," Joe tells her with a reassuring smile. Then, echoing the words he has heard his superiors use to patients' families, he adds in a strong voice, "We have every reason now to be optimistic."

Mrs. Roberts's face is suddenly suffused with naked joy and relief. "Oh, thank you, Dr. Dasher, thank you." Her gratitude is so intense, her reverence so visible, that she seems about to kiss his ring.

And so the young physician, buoyed by this incredible boost to his ego, squares his shoulders proudly and continues on his rounds.

Every room he enters contains patients and families eagerly awaiting his arrival. "How am I, doc?" "What were the results of her test, doctor?" "Why does he feel that pain in his side?" "When can we take her home?" Their fates rest in his hands and they hang on his every word. For is he not the giver of life down here on earth? Is he not the sole repository of hope for cure? At that moment in time their lives depend on him; no matter who they are out in the world—in here he is their superior.

This is very heady stuff for a young man who has until recently led a book-bound, sheltered academic life. It is a flattery he is unable to resist, and Joe soon begins to respond to his patients' deference and, worse yet, begins to accept it as his due—and the deification process begins.

From the moment a medical school graduate puts on that white coat and walks among the patients bearing answers to their life-and-death questions he becomes an instant god. It was a role Joe slipped into, tentatively at first, then firmly when he realized the patients needed it—demanded it. When a person is lying in a hospital bed ill and desperately frightened, the fulcrum of his and his family's existence is his health. Wars, nuclear blasts, emotional problems, and career questions all recede into unreality and irrelevance. Their world is The Hospital. Their sole interest is: Will our loved one live or die? Will he get better and when?

The only one who can answer their questions is the doctor. The only one who can furnish the passport out of the world of the sick is the doctor.

To them he is God.

This was a posture Joe Dasher had a bit of difficulty adjusting to at first, but the exaltation of being an infallible deity was too alluring to resist for long and he soon succumbed. It didn't take much time for the role to become reality and for Joe to truly believe that he was a fantastic, powerful, and elite human being.

For his young wife, Karen, the transformation was something she witnessed with perplexity, then impatience, then anger.

Joe and Karen met in New York City, where Karen had come after she had graduated from a college in the Midwest. "He was so sweet, and such fun." They fell in love and Joe wanted to get married at once before he started medical school. But Karen was hesitant. She came from a small town where she had seen the loneliness of a doctor's wife. "I want a companion, not just a husband," she told him. "Doctors are never home." Joe assured her they would have time together—that physicians these days lead a more ordinary and less demanding existence than the small-town GP of years ago. And so they were married. Their son, Timmy, was born during Joe's third year of school.

"I thought the medical school years were bad. He was always exhausted and had no time for Timmy and me. But at least the hours we did spend together were wonderful, and he enjoyed the simple pleasures—baking cookies together, going to the park. He loved to hear about Timmy's shenanigans. But the internship and residency changed him completely. Once he entered the hospital we lost him. He became an unreachable god."

When Joe came home it was merely to sleep. Awake he was so full of himself that Karen found him unapproachable and insufferable. Details of his family's life were of little interest to him. He became impatient with Karen if she recounted some of the little successes and minor crises that fill the home day—Timmy's sandbox victory over a bully, Karen's exasperating confrontation with the plumber. Joe brushed these aside as nonsense unworthy of his attention.

"Timmy and I were unimportant to him. Of course what happened to us were minor incidents in the scheme of things. How could we compete on the life-value scale with a woman dying of a brain tumor or a child unable to talk because of a glioma? The patients' families look upon Joe as a god, but to me he was a man."

Karen felt she could not compete with the hospital. This passage from the book *Brain Surgeon* best describes her problem.

> The training left little time and less energy for things beyond the hospital. . . . When you spend that much time with people who needed you, it could be awfully hard to be with those who didn't. The great temptation was to hang around the hospital, extend your schedule until the time beyond it was only for sleep, and the more you succumbed to this, the less life you had outside, the more reason you had to stick around the ward. If you spent time with doctors, you could sympathize with their problem. It was uncanny how quickly I [the writer] came to feel like them myself. I wasn't needed by anyone here, but after a couple of weeks around the hospital, life outside began to seem pale and diffuse by comparison. It didn't matter that the events I witnessed might be devastating. I found myself reluctant to leave, rushing back, stopping by on weekends. If I was a junky in such a short time, imagine the habit with which the doctors had to contend.

Karen tried to get Joe into a discussion about her feelings—the fears she felt of what she saw as an incipiently dangerous deterioration of their marriage. But she found him consistently unwilling to talk. The time he spent at home was merely to fill his physical needs—eating, changing clothes, making sure she had sent his shirts to the laundry, sleeping, and sex. The first few times Karen brought up the subject of the unsatisfactory state of their marriage Joe reacted with impatience and then anger. "He saw it as all my fault; I was being emotional, unreasonable, and demanding," said Karen. "After all, how could he be wrong— he was the great godlike doctor."

Subsequently whenever she tried to bring up the subject,

he would find a reason to leave the house. "The hospital called or he had to make rounds or attend a meeting. Doctors have more excuses for leaving home than men in any other profession," said Karen ruefully.

The problem was that Joe found himself reveling in his new position of power. The hospital became the most rewarding, fulfilling part of his existence and at the first sign of any difficulty in any other facet of his life, any area where his self-image was at risk, he would escape to the hospital, where patients and patients' families would give him the ego support he needed. As Karen called it, he was going to get his "God-fix." As soon as Karen accused him of an inability to communicate he retorted, "That's your problem, not mine. I've been communicating satisfactorily all day with doctors, nurses, and patients."

Faced with that kind of reaction and response, Karen began to doubt herself. Maybe she was too demanding. Perhaps her expectations were unrealistic. But the loneliness, the sense of betrayal, was consuming. He had promised her that his career ambitions would never interfere with his love and respect for her and the needs of their marriage. He had insisted that his family would always be the most important portion of his life.

Karen felt she had been had in every sense of the word. Even their sex life had become perfunctory; Joe seemed to regard their home as a personal service station—a place to fill his needs at his convenience.

Fortunately, Karen was a strong, independent woman who would not accept this treatment without a battle. She finally presented Joe with an ultimatum: "Either we go for counseling or I leave you." Faced with that choice, Joe opted for therapy.

Joe was made to realize that the daily reverence he received was directed toward his professional, not his total, being. He realized that the deity role must be doffed at home as the carryover was destructive to any normal family relationship. And most of all, when threatened with the imminent loss of Karen and Timmy, he realized their importance to him. Karen and Joe worked out an understanding of each other's needs—she was made to appreciate the intensely emotional demands his profession imposed on him and his need for home quiet time, and he was made to realize that his dealings with life-and-death situations did not minimize the importance of the daily emotional minutiae that occurred to his wife and child.

Karen was firm enough in her self-belief to fight for the survival of her marriage on mutually satisfactory terms. But what about the thousands of doctors' wives who do not have that strength?

More than any other question in the *Medical/Mrs.* questionnaire, the question, "Do you suffer due to the 'God' status your husband enjoys?" touched a mainspring of misery among the 100,000 doctors' wives and evoked an outpouring of letters indicating that many are suffering with husbands whose godlike postures make normal marital relationships impossible.

> I married a "surgeon"—not a "human" man. Our marriage suffered. He's trying now to meet my needs but I've learned to satisfy them myself and really don't *need* him anymore. Are other surgeons like this? Or would my husband have been the same if he were a shoe salesman? In any event, I wouldn't have married a shoe salesman—and a shoe salesman probably wouldn't have the same grand ego needs of a surgeon. (Virginia)

> This doctor is absolutely faithful, trustworthy, honest— a pillar of society—but inflexible, egotistical, unbending with me. (Brooklyn, N.Y.)

These women are living lives of emotional deprivation, made all the worse by the fact that everywhere they go they encounter adoring patients who tell them how marvelous their husbands are. The inescapable conclusion each of these women must reach is: "If he's so fantastic, the fault must be mine."

In an article in the *American Medical News* (Sept. 22, 1978), "Adored at the office—Abhorred at home," the process of patient adulation that leads to the wreck of a happy home is described:

As "fast-answer" men, doctors can get lulled into thinking they have all the answers. If Mrs. Jones complains of diarrhea, you tell her you'll phone in a prescription for her and to phone back in the morning. If Mr. Smith has severe chest pains, you tell him to meet you right away at the hospital.

All day long you have answers for practically everything. As an esteemed member of the community, your opinion is also highly regarded on many nonmedical issues.

On top of "having all the answers," a doctor gets little, if any, honest feedback about himself from anyone he works with. . . .

Certainly in most hospitals, nurses are excessively polite, supportive, and even submissive to doctors. By and large, nurses wouldn't dream of yelling back at a doctor or telling him off. Rather, it's "Oh, yes, doctor, I'm sure that'll be just fine," or "Thank you very much, doctor. We'll do that right away."

Likewise, it is a rare administrator who would risk losing a doctor's business by being anything but solicitous, no matter how unreasonable a doctor may be.

The situation in a doctor's own office resembles a pyramid with the doctor sitting on top. He is The Boss, the sole reason for everyone's being there, including the patient.

Then, too, a doctor is unlikely to fall out with a colleague, unless there is absolutely no chance of exchanging referrals. Most doctors, at least on the surface, remain friendly with each other.

The only other people with whom a doctor comes in

daily contact during business hours are his patients, who are usually respectful and adoring. Even if a patient doesn't like his doctor or is less than satisfied with the treatment, he will probably not speak up nor is he likely to rebuke his doctor with anything like "I think you could have been supportive of my mother while my father was dying of cancer."

If a patient does switch doctors, the chances are slim that he will tell his former doctor why he is leaving. More likely, he will just leave, thus becoming an "ungrateful patient" as far as the doctor is concerned. . . .

So there you have it. Throughout the day, the doctor is surrounded by people boosting his ego and rarely, if ever, questioning his competence or modus operandi. What an excellent setup for nurturing the God complex.

If you take the doctor out of this work situation, where there is little criticism and a whole lot of power, and place him back home where the issues are more mundane and where he is simply John Doe married to Jane Doe, it is no wonder there may be trouble. It is not an easy transition to make.

However, the home may be the one place where the doctor can get his feet on the ground. If there is a good marital relationship, a doctor's wife may offer constructive feedback lacking elsewhere, and the husband will probably listen.

On the other hand, the wife may see that things are not going well in the marriage but may think that it is her fault, and that the best thing to do is to keep her mouth shut. After all, everyone else tells her how great her husband is. He is a lionized member of the community, a doctor. The more she hears how terrific he is, the more depressed she feels. She wonders, "How come I can't get along with him?"

In the current climate of women's consciousness raising and self-actualization, young wives are speaking up more and are refusing to live with the less in a marital relationship that their mothers and grandmothers were conditioned to accept. But for women who have been married to doctors for many years, this "revolution" has come too late.

For Evelyn L., who has been married to a physician for twenty-three years, "The greatest problem is his need for admiration and adulation and inability to accept the fact that I also have human psychological needs. In a nutshell, I feel my husband thinks women are mainly as supportive for man/husband/doctor."

Most of these women have suffered in silence. They are unable to complain to friends. For one thing, there is the risk of damaging their husbands' positions in the community. After all, it does not suit the image of the omnipotent healer to be shown to be unable to handle the needs of his own family. Furthermore, the doctor's wife is a much envied person. By conventional measurements she has all the accoutrements of the good life—money, social position. Her children attend good schools, she lives well in an upper-class milieu. While many of her friends and their husbands are working desperately to keep ahead of inflation and to meet mounting payments for college, food, rent, she has nothing to do but spend her time disposing of her husband's huge disposable income. How can she complain to anyone and expect them to evince any sympathy for her psyche? So she's not happy . . . who's happy? How miserable can you be as you toss your Vuitton bag on the seat of your Mercedes on the way to your club?

Yet the depth of her emotional anguish is intense and all the more so because of the guilt she feels in feeling miserable. She knows she has all the societal stamps of success . . . she knows her husband is regarded as a superbeing and she should be proud of being Mrs. Superbeing. But can all this compensate for the sense of abandonment and frustration she feels?

In a study called "The Doctor's Wife: Mental Illness

and Marital Pattern" (1975 *International Journal of Psychiatry in Medicine*) it was observed that "it is a clinical impression that physicians' wives present in disproportionately large numbers as patients; that in the vast majority, severe marital problems are present; and that the marital relationship shows a similar pattern."

As they pointed out, "Typically the physician's wife presents as depressed, angry, and desperately unhappy. Frequently she is bewildered as to why she is experiencing such feelings. Materially comfortable with secure social status, usually a financially generous husband and often envied, her unhappiness and anger may seem inappropriate to her."

But the fact is those feelings are there. How to deal with them has been one of the major problems of medical marriages—one that has finally reached an area of open recognition.

During the last few years, articles and studies on the difficulties in medical marriages have cropped up steadily in medical journals: "Psychiatric Illness in the Physician's Wife"; "The Doctor and His Marriage"; "Marital Stability among Physicians"; "Doctors and Divorce: Who's at Risk?"; "The Physician's Marriage"; "Divorce among Doctors"; "Doctor and Mrs.: Their Mental Health." These are just some of the titles that are emerging with a regularity that indicates the problem is now out in the open. Even the AMA, which dedicates itself to the proposition that though all men may be created equal, somewhere along the way doctors get to be better than equal . . . even this august organization has become defensive about the accusations that physicians make less than perfect husbands.

The September 1979 issue of *Facets*, the magazine published for ladies of the AMA auxiliaries, contained the following articles: "Is the Story of the Unhappy Doctor's

Spouse Myth or Reality?"; "Phil Donahue Show Gets Spirited Defense of Medical Marriages"; "The Physician's Marriage: Joys and Sorrows."

What is apparent is that the medical community, which previously held itself as infallible on all fronts, is now acknowledging possible weakness, at least in the human relations area. With the current trend to let everything hang out, unhappy doctors' wives are coming out of the closet in droves.

After discovering that fully one quarter of his patients were doctors' wives, psychiatrist Philip A. Barrata, Jr., created a course at the University of California called "Physician's Wife—No Bed of Roses."

"People listen to what a doctor has to say with great deference then go to his wife and say, 'What a great husband you have,'" observes Dr. Barrata. "What is she supposed to answer—that this is the same man who forgot to pick up his underwear that morning?"

The course has been so successful that Dr. Barrata will introduce two more courses: "Doctor as Spouse and Parent—So Little Time" and "Balancing the Demands of Family Life and Medical Practice."

Ten years ago, Dr. Barrata's courses would have been unthinkable; what self-respecting doctor's wife would openly admit the doctor's failure as husband? Today, however, there are seminars, symposiums, and AMA meetings on the subject. The position of the doctor was unassailable, his image so deific, that endowing him with mortal weaknesses was unthinkable. But now iconoclasm has become a public passion. We either strike down our idols or reduce them to the approachable category of mere men.

Inevitably men of medicine have become prime targets of this sentiment. The rash of malpractice suits is symptomatic of the new rush to question. There are no absolutes anymore—we recognize no sacred cows. If ever a time was

ripe for doctors' wives to air complaints and confess that
life with these gods is filled with human pain and error,
that time is now.

When but now would a magazine receive letters like
these from doctors' wives?

My husband gets much positive feedback—compliments
from nurses, patients, other physicians which constantly
feed his ego. A doctor's wife has much more expected from
her than other wives without getting much emotional support or positive feedback. We have no one to tell us how
well we handle patients on the phone, children on lonely
weekends and evenings. We can't rely on our husbands for
anything.

A disillusioned doctor's wife from New Jersey expressed
her deep unhappiness:

My husband is still a very loving person but only on his
terms. His practice comes first. He has a sincere interest
in family but prefers to not have his energies required in
family matters. He feels his role is outside the home and
my role is in the home. I am tired of changing my goals
so that he is happy, tired of trying to make up for his
broken promises to others, tired of making excuses for
absences, tired of waiting to develop a relationship. First it
was "wait until I've finished this residency," then "wait
until I have the practice established." Now it's "wait until
I have this partnership established and this office expansion completed." The last seven years since he began private practice have been horrible. The strange thing is that
no one would surmise that I am miserable. If I were to
initiate a sensitive discussion with him I would be told,
"I don't need problems when I come home. I hear people's
problems all day. When you give me problems at home
it affects my work, my performance in surgery (the old
guilt trick!). I have to go check on some people at the
hospital." He leaves then until he knows *everyone* will be
asleep at home.

Among unhappy doctors' wives, perhaps the ones who have the roughest time are those married to psychiatrists. It is hard to overcome the sense of failure a woman feels when her marriage isn't working—hard for her to convince herself that her spouse bears at least some if not all of the responsibility. But when that husband is a psychiatrist, fixing blame and guilt becomes very one-sided indeed; that's his department and he handles the job like a skilled professional. Some women face the special difficulties of living with a psychiatrist with humor, as evidenced in this poem, which appeared in the *Nova Scotia Medical Journal*:

Lament of the Wife of a Psychiatrist

I never get mad: I get hostile;
I never feel sad: I'm depressed.
If I sew or I knit and enjoy it a bit,
I'm not handy—I'm merely obsessed.

I never regret—I feel guilty,
And if I should vacuum the hall,
Wash the woodwork and such, and not mind it too much,
Am I tidy? Compulsive is all.

If I can't choose a hat, I have conflicts,
With ambivalent feelings about net,
I never get worried or nervous or hurried:
Anxiety—that's what I get.

If I'm too happy, I must be euphoric;
If I go to the Stork Club or Ritz
And have a good time making puns or rhyme,
I'm a manic, or maybe a schiz.

If I tell you you're right, I'm submissive,
Repressing aggressiveness, too,
And when I disagree, I'm defensive, you see,
And projecting my symptoms on you.

I love you, but that's just transference
With Oedipus rearing his head.

My breathing asthmatic is psychosomatic,
A fear of exclaiming "Drop dead!"
I'm not lonely, simply dependent.
My dog has no fleas, just a tic.
So if I seem cad, never mind just be glad
That I'm not a stinker, I'm sick.

                                    SONYA SAROYAN

But not every wife is able to be so sanguine about the difficulties of dealing with the often insufferably omniscient attitudes of a psychoanalyst, for the psychiatrist's wife bears the unique burden of living with a man who can explain away all her complaints with a clinical evaluation that places all the onus on her. No matter how positive she may be about the reasons for her unhappiness, no matter how sure she is that certain elements in his behavior are causing her pain, that belief must be shaken by his "professional assessment" of the "real" motivations and psychological aberrations behind her demands. After all, he is a respected analytic practitioner and there must be some shred of validity in his diagnosis. It should be illegal for a psychoanalyst to use his professional training as weapons in a fight, just as a prizefighter's fists are classified as lethal weapons.

There is strong public awareness today of the tragedy of battered wives. Physical abuse is deplorable, but what about psychological abuse? Is not the battering of the psyche equally painful and destructive?

The most agonizing problem of the battered wife is her inability to find a method of exit from the marriage. Besides the emotional attachment, the usual chain that binds her is financial; he is the sole source of family support, she has no money of her own—where can she go and how can she maintain herself and children?

We usually associate this difficulty with lower income groups. But the same constraint exists in a higher income situation where the wife, having become accustomed to a superior standard of living, finds withdrawal from the marriage would impose financial penalties that would drop her below these acceptable levels. A psychologically battered psychiatrist's wife from Scarsdale can be locked into an untenable marriage by the same fiscal fears that paralyze a physically battered spouse in Hamtramack.

Ethel and Martin Moore were married in their early twenties, when they were both graduate students in Boston, where he was in medical school and she was getting an advanced degree in art history. Ethel was competent academically, but in areas of pragmatic living her approach was unrealistic and immature. Brought up by indulgent parents who supported her totally, Ethel had no awareness of financial pressures or the harsh realities of making a living. Martin was a brilliant, extremely practical and ambitious young man, the very antithesis of Ethel. He was charmed by her soft naïveté and slightly unworldly air. Her obvious need to be "looked after" appealed to his strong need to be "big daddy."

As was so often the case in those years, helplessness was associated with femininity, and assertive bluster that masked the neurotic need to control was regarded as masculine. And so they were married. During the school years, when they both worked part time to support themselves, Martin was perfectly willing to do his share of the domestic chores, especially the marketing, where he felt Ethel's impracticality made her a poor shopper. At first they had a joint checking account, but when he discovered that Ethel wrote checks without any attempt to balance the account because her mother always covered what she wrote, Martin took over the finances . . . a pattern that was to be a permanent one in their marriage. Ethel did not object when he changed the account to his name only. In fact, she was relieved. Whenever she needed money, she asked Martin, and if he approved, she got it.

The pattern of dominance and submission was established early in their relationship and it worked well for both of them for many years.

Then the children came and Martin established an extremely lucrative psychiatric practice in a major West Coast city. They moved to a lovely house and Ethel settled happily into the existence of a suburban housewife and mother of two sons. Her life responsibilities were minimal; Martin paid the bills, chose where and when they would vacation, made all the important decisions. She looked after the home and the boys, and played golf. Her weekly allowance and store charge cards kept her totally happy, except that every now and then she would become angry at the demands Martin imposed. He had to have entertainment provided for him every Saturday night—and that was her job. After all, he spent his days sitting and listening to people . . . didn't he need the stimulation of social exchange on the weekend? Since their social life was one of the few responsibilities assigned to Ethel, she would become desperate toward the end of the week if there was no event scheduled for Saturday night and would frantically call friends to invite them to a dinner party. Every few months she would rebel in a childlike fury and there would be screaming accusations of tyranny and selfishness. His answer would be, "I have extremely strong needs and they must be met." He also pointed out that she was living a delightfully easy life, and his expectations from her were hardly excessive—a well-run home, cleaned and pressed clothing (he liked his cotton knit tennis shirts and all socks ironed), and he provided her with a full-time maid.

This husband-wife/parent-child relationship continued for twenty-five years, stormy, but to the obvious satisfaction of both partners. And then two things occurred to change the status quo: The last child left home for college, and the women's liberation movement began.

Suddenly the house was lonely and empty; Ethel's sense

of purpose was gone. Martin came home at exactly 6:30 every evening as always, and dinner was on the table at 6:45. But mealtime became somewhat desultory. No excitement provided by the children's recounting of activities of the day, what was there for the two of them to talk about? Soon, Martin began coming home later—and suddenly announced that Wednesday evenings he would be having dinner downtown.

Although she had absolutely no substantiation, Ethel became convinced that Martin was having an affair: If he arrived home at 6:45 instead of 6:30, she attacked him with accusations and vilification. Dinnertime became an occasion for harangues that ended with Martin stalking away from the table and going to his study to read—behind a closed door. Totally unable to control herself, Ethel poured out her complaints to everyone she knew, friends, casual acquaintances, and, worst of all, her children. And their friends, sympathetic at first, began to lose patience and avoid her. She was miserable, but how else could she react? Shielded and indulged all her life—first by her parents and then by her husband—Helen was unable to handle adversity with any other than infantile tantrum-style behavior.

Then as some of the issues of the women's movement started to reach her, she began to believe that every woman should have some degree of independence. Perhaps she should leave Martin and strike out on her own. Encouraged by friends, she decided that this would be her only route to self-respect. It was then that she realized that she had no money; everything she thought they owned was in Martin's name. Completely dependent on him always, a role he encouraged, she had never involved herself in their financial affairs. Now she discovered herself to be totally without resources. Her infantilization was indeed complete. The realization drove her into a fury of impotent rage. She demanded money from Martin—a bank account of her own so that she could feel like a partner not a chattel. Martin refused; as always, he would continue to give her what funds she needed if he deemed it a necessary expenditure.

Money had always been a tool used by Martin to exert control over Ethel and their children, and he saw no reason to discontinue a method he found very satisfactory. Ethel felt locked in; she knew that a divorce would reduce her standard of living drastically. Besides, she was afraid of freedom—where would she go; how could she cope with life? Here she was in middle age unable to handle finances, unaware of how to deal with anything but the simplest elements of self-maintenance. The submissive relationship that Martin had developed and nurtured because it suited his needs and self-image—and she fostered because it was a continuation of a role she had always enjoyed—was now a massive trap for Ethel. Her feelings and needs had changed. Unfortunately, maturity had arrived late in her life and she no longer wanted to pay the trade-off price for security that suited her in earlier years.

She had driven herself into a corner. Although she hated her life as it was, she was too fearful of the unknown to risk making a sortie into the world on her own. In despair and frustration she kept striking out at Martin and was in a constant state of anger. But it was ineffective, for although Ethel desperately needed a new structure to their marital relationship, Martin did not. The pattern they had established suited him just fine and he saw no reason to alter it in any way. True, he found her outbursts bothersome, but he looked upon them as menopausal behavior that she would outgrow. And when her ranting and raving became too annoying Martin would hand her a tranquilizer and tell her coolly, "Take this—you're having a psychotic episode."

Martin's method of dealing with Ethel's unhappiness is consistent with the doctor's self-image of infallibility. *She* was being unreasonable, *she* was having a psychotic episode.

She would need psychotherapy (which he ultimately dispatched her into). The doctor is never at fault—after all, can God err?

Today Ethel is in her second year of therapy but very little has changed. Although she claims she now has the strength and resolve to get a divorce, she has taken no concrete steps to obtain one. Martin is not happy with Ethel's sniping and surly behavior but has adjusted to it. Their relationship has evolved into a state of harmonious hostility which seems to serve both their needs.

If a man trained in psychiatric medicine comes to see himself as the omnipotent seer who comprehends the inner workings of the mind and can influence human behavior, think of the self-image of the neurosurgeon who has direct and immediate effect on the physical survival of his patients. The role of God becomes as natural to him as breathing and must eventually take over all aspects of his life. Marriage to such a man presents a specific sort of hell that a wife must come to terms with or crack. This letter from a young neurosurgeon's wife hints at the difficulties:

> The biggest problem is my husband's failure to realize that while he may be "God" at the hospital and his word is law—that different expectations are encompassed in a healthy family relationship. He tends to give orders to me and our children—we all resent this. Though he recognizes the problem and always tries to make up for his errant behavior, it is very difficult (understatement) living with him. He is a neurosurgeon and I *do* understand the pressure he faces in the operating room—BUT I'm thirty six years old now, my children 11 & 12 and I'm getting tired of the whole routine. Until I can find a better way out . . . I tend to ignore him a lot.

She will be hard pressed to "find a better way out." Since neurosurgeons spend the bulk of their time playing the

part of God, they find it most difficult to switch over to the
roles of ordinary man, husband, and father when they cross
the home threshold.

A day spent with one of these special geniuses of the knife,
as described in *Brain Surgeon*, gives a clear insight into the
problems of living with such a man.

> "You get used to it," said Dr. Brockman. "We play God
> every day." It was an old cliché and he (the neurosurgeon)
> was of course making fun of it. What was odd and a little
> frightening, was that for a moment it seemed not exces-
> sively grandiose. One man (the patient) was stalked by
> untimely death and another had set out to stop his clock.
> Brockman did his best to to keep this part of his work in
> perspective but it was seductive. For obvious reasons the
> patients liked to believe him omnipotent and it isn't easy
> to play that role if you don't believe in it yourself. As
> Brockman put it once when someone attacked him for
> confusing himself with God, "Who do you want mess-
> ing around in your brain—someone who think's he's a
> plumber?"

The self-absorption basic in such a personality becomes a
tremendous obstacle to the give and take required in the
growth of a family relationship. A man who views himself
as supremely successful, having reached the pinnacle of
power in the life-and-death control he exerts, has no motivation to expand his interests and horizons, or to accommodate himself to the needs of others. Why should he?
Every day his sense of superiority is reinforced by the attitudes of patients, patients' families, nurses, and others
who regard him with admiration bordering on worship.

But this steady feeding of the ego becomes like a drug
and he can't go "cold turkey" when the workday ends.
Which is why the leisure pursuits of surgeons tend toward
activities that offer strong challenges and the chance to conquer and prove oneself over and over again. Dr. Joseph

Ransohoff, the famed neurosurgeon, spends his vacations and weekends fishing for shark. He loves taking his boat out in bad weather and coming in by instruments. Dr. Anthony Imparato, the renowned vascular surgeon, travels by two planes and boats to a remote camp in Greenland to fish for salmon. Of the surgical staff surveyed at New York University Medical Center, 33 percent of the surgeons were serious fishermen and 22 percent were competitive squash or racket-ball players.

Note that these activities require a minimum of social exchange. The intellectual growth that evolves from exploring new ideas and the personality growth that develops with exposures to different people are not part of the surgeon's maturation. The process of building a self-image evolves from the reception one receives from others and the adjustments made along the way to correct and improve these responses. When a developing adult notices that certain actions or statements set off unpleasant reactions in others, his basic desire to be liked will induce some behavior modification. He'll try to change, he'll want to be nicer. But a surgeon does not have these opportunities. Almost ALL his relationships are on a God/mortal basis, and as stated in the *American Medical News* article, "A doctor gets little, if any, honest feedback about himself." Thus he is never given any motivation to alter his behavior in any way. Why change? Everyone thinks he's marvelous . . . he thinks.

Pity his poor wife. Not limited by this character-growth block that surgeons encounter, she moves away from him in many different directions. As pointed out by Dr. Alan Morganstern, a Portland, Oregon, psychiatrist who counsels many physicians and their wives, doctors often marry women with a greater breadth of emotional expression than their own. The surgeon's wife wants to explore new disciplines, she is interested in learning and expanding her social and intellectual horizons, and like most halves of couples, she looks to share these experiences with her spouse. But her husband has no such interests or desires. His needs are being thoroughly fulfilled daily—he is smugly satisfied with himself and sees no reason for incursions into new spheres. The usual result of such a schism in a marital relationship is discussion and compromise . . . talking things out and each one bending a bit to please the other.

But a surgeon does not bend. Accustomed to the management of power and the all-or-nothing aspects of its decisions, the surgical personality is intransigent. The most frequent complaint heard from surgeons' wives was the lack of compromise and consideration they learned to expect from their husbands. His almost total intractability and the need to create a single life of her own in order to survive was the standard.

Ruth and David were married right after college graduation. David's relentless pursuit of Ruth was flattering and compelling and gave some intimation of the single-minded persistence that was later to bring him international renown as one of the most highly skilled and innovative neurosurgeons in the world.

They came from similar privileged backgrounds in the same Midwestern city—luxurious homes, country clubs, ivy league colleges. But their personalities were totally dissimilar. Ruth was artistic, intellectual, and gentle, traits that David found utterly charming. David was rebellious, iconoclastic, and competitive, qualities that Ruth found somewhat fascinating. The match was highly approved by both families and the wedding was a major social event. Everyone regarded them as eminently suited for one another and the marriage according to conventional standards had all the prescribed ingredients for absolute success. Since David came from a long line of eminent physicians, it was a natural step for him to apply to medical school and, of course, be accepted. They moved to the large eastern city where the school was located and settled at once into the regulation marital bliss which included having two children within four years. But then the overachiever aspect of David's character went into high gear. Medical school and internship and residency were consuming enough, but David *had* to be the best in his class, tops in his group, the most effective member of the team. This continuing effort exacted a tremendous toll on him and his family. The children rarely saw their father. Family dinner inevitably ended in a close-to-tears mommy standing at the window watching for the daddy that never showed. Each time David reached an aspired-for plateau, Ruth hoped that this would be *it*, he would now be satisfied and they could settle into a normal home life.

But that never occurred because there were always more goals, more peaks for David to conquer. Ruth found it difficult to fault him because the pursuit of excellence is a highly regarded quality in our society and ambition in a young man is considered a commendable asset. But Ruth suffered, and began to wonder at what point does the compulsion to excel cross from the bounds of attribute into the neurosis of obsession? She remembered her happy, parent-surrounded childhood, with a father who enjoyed regular working hours, where dinner en famille was the high point of the evening when everyone chattered joyfully about the personal happenings of the day.

She thought longingly of the many childhood trips and picnics and visiting excursions that compromised the fabric of a close-knit family life and tried to organize similar activities with David and their children. But either David said no, or worse—said yes and then forgot or called to cancel. When he came home one day and announced he had bought a boat, Ruth was overjoyed: Here was the chance for parents and children to spend solid time together—on the water—away from the phones and pull of the hospital . . . carefree, intimate, just a relaxed experience and chance to enjoy each other. But her fantasy was short-

lived; she had reckoned without David's compulsively perfectionist character. He could not just have a pleasure boat,
it had to be the best and the fastest. The children were too
young to function as crew and their nonseafaring behavior
was a constant irritant to the new captain. David would not
permit them to have cookies or potato chips, or eat any
messy food for fear their carelessness would mean greasy
fingerprints on the teak decks. Their visits to "the head" had
to be closely monitored for fear they would stuff more than
the four-square allotment of toilet paper into the plumbing.
Each boating trip, far from being a joy, was a nerve-racking nightmare in which Ruth spent her time alternately
trying to keep the children out of David's way and calming
their tears after one of David's explosions of abuse at some
of their violations of his rules. It was finally apparent to
Ruth that her idea of the function of the boat was totally
different from David's: Where she saw it as a source of
family fun and togetherness, he saw it as a vehicle of solitary
escape from the rigors of his pressure-packed days and nights.
What he wanted was to be alone—all alone.

They had a huge emotionally charged fight where Ruth
finally accused David of total self-involvement and consuming neurotic need to prove himself constantly at all
costs—namely her and the children. She demanded that
they see a therapist together, and he agreed.

The course of therapy was helpful and cruelly revealing to
Ruth. David admitted openly to being driven and compulsive, but stated emphatically that he would never change.
He loved his wife and children, but his need to constantly
push for new heights of achievement in his profession was
an obsession that transcended all other considerations in his
life. He gave Ruth no choice but to accept the marriage on
his terms or not at all.

Ruth had some painful thinking and evaluations to make.
The questions were: Did she love and want David enough
to be willing to live the sort of life his needs dictated? Would

she be able to cope with the fact that she and their children would always occupy a secondary position in David's considerations? And could she face the reality that compromises in her marriage would always be strictly unilateral and deal with the unfairness of it all without resentment and anger? Ruth realized that her marriage would never provide her with the warmth and companionship that she had anticipated. She knew that her husband did not share in her interests in art, archaeology, history, and theater, but she had hoped he would at least attempt to participate in some of her activities for her sake, just as she attended conventions and meetings and entertained his colleagues and staff. Now she had to accept the reality that he saw no reason to accommodate to her needs or desires. He was telling her quite clearly and openly: I have no wish to be a great husband and a great father, just a great neurosurgeon. Take me as I am, warts and all, or not at all.

Ruth made her decision. She realized that she loved and respected David, and could not see herself living without him. She would have to accept his terms. But in order to survive, she knew it was vital that she find an area of self-fulfillment that did not involve David. Living forever in his professional shadow would be dangerously destructive and she must find a career of her own. Since her liberal arts education prepared her for only the most esoteric pursuits, she sought counseling to investigate areas of potential professional opportunities. Her compassion and talent for dealing with people pointed toward psychology and she enrolled in a full-time master's degree program in a nearby college, arranging her hours to be home when the children arrived home from school. After graduation, Ruth was accepted on the psychiatric social work staff of a large hospital and began a career in which she gradually rose to a position of active importance.

It was the salvation of their marriage and of Ruth's life. She developed friendships that filled the voids left by

David's unwillingness to extend himself in any way. Since traveling was something Ruth loved, she look trips with cultural groups and with friends. She became an independent being and derived deep personal satisfaction from that knowledge. Their marriage now worked well because it encompassed three different lives—his, hers, and theirs.

There are times when Ruth explodes in resentment at David's implacability, especially when she encounters a couple who live a close companionable existence and her envy provokes sorrow and anger. It passes because Ruth made her peace and her bargain long ago. But she sometimes wonders if the price was not too high.

IV

Family Life—
What Family Life?

As they passed the big-city hospital where his father worked, six-year-old Tod Green asked his mother, "Is that where Daddy lives?"

To the doctor's child, the hospital represents an amorphous competitor—a threatening massive unknown that takes Daddy away from the house constantly; to the doctor's wife, it represents an unfair rival who offers her husband an exciting escape hatch he can take whenever he gets bored, or bothered with home life.

"David loves his children, but he doesn't take any responsibility. I do all the disciplining," says Ann S., wife of an Atlanta physician. "He wants to come home and have peace and quiet. If there is bickering, he will just get up from the dinner table and announce that he has to go to the hospital to make rounds. It's infuriating to me and the kids that he won't get involved with their problems at all—but what can we do? How can we fight the hospital?"

The doctor's family may have a deep-rooted suspicion he is using the call of his profession as a convenient alibi to avoid the responsibility of relationships with his wife and children. But how can they prove it? And worse, how can they complain? As Betty S., wife of a California orthopedic surgeon, said, "When Sam tells us he has to see to the needs of a man who just got busted up on the freeway, how can I bitch about the fact that he's taking off in the middle of an unpleasant discussion with our daughter about her sexual activities? I suspect he just wants out—he hates facing up to Susie's problems—but there's that poor guy in agony in the hospital and Sam says he has to go. Sure I resent his leaving me to handle the whole mess, but the frustrating thing for me is—I have no one to really get mad at!"

Betty's suspicion that her husband is seeking to avoid facing up to family difficulties is buttressed by research that shows physicians are often unable to give of themselves emotionally. In a study conducted by Vaillant, Sobowale, and McArthur reported in the *New England Journal of Medicine*, it was found that physicians tend to rely more heavily on defense mechanisms such as denial, masochism, and passive aggressive behavior, "vehement aversion to some instinctively gratifying behavior and often the substitution of an opposite behavior. . . . Some physicians seemed almost phobic about asking for help." The study goes on to point out what many psychiatrists have often suspected: "Some physicians may elect to assume direct care of patients to give others the care they did not receive in their own childhood," and for such doctors the practice of medicine will indeed become a stress when they are asked to give more, in an emotional sense, than they themselves have been given.

But even more crippling is the authoritarian role the doctor is assigned, a position that makes it difficult for him to handle the kind of defiant behavior one gets from adolescent offspring. A physician suffers from "role-strain," according to the *Journal of Social Psychiatry*: "The role requires that a doctor function at a maximum level of competence at all times." The expectation of perfect performance lays a heavy burden on the physician that he may not feel adequate to handle. When his wife and children present him with problems and turn to him for solutions, the strain of living up to his own fantasy as wisdom incarnate gets to be too much to bear—and he resorts to anger or absentia, both highly destructive elements in familial relationships.

Perhaps worse is the reaction of the doctor who has been seduced by society into truly believing he is infallible, that he is in fact qualified to operate superbly and flaw-free in all areas of life. And it's so easy for such a self-delusion to grow. The interaction between patient and physician tends to bring out authoritarian feelings of superior knowledge and ability in the doctor. "I'm sick—I depend on you to cure me. I believe you have the answer." And when the patient recovers, either due to the ministrations of the doctor or more often because of the naturally powerful recuperative powers of the body, the doctor gets the credit. The patient points with pride to his great healer and the superior image of the doctor is reinforced.

Now puffed up with pride and self-importance, the grateful thanks of his patient still ringing in his ears, he heads home, crosses the threshold, and all hell breaks loose. Suddenly he is confronted with a surly teenager who sneers at his authority. And a wife who is distraught because the school guidance counselor has advised her that their daughter's PSAT scores wouldn't even qualify her for a two-year community college. Now he's faced with problems that cannot be neatly and scientifically solved with prescriptions, advice, or surgery. And instead of deferential patients who ask for his advice and follow it to the letter, he is dealing with rebellious children who are angered by his imperious attitude, resentful of his frequent absences, and totally unresponsive to any advice he offers. Life has not equipped him to handle these sorts of crises and his ego cannot cope with the punishment. So he tells his wife that she must handle things since he has a number of ill patients he must visit.

Under the circumstances, is this behavior surprising? To start, the doctor is usually, as research has indicated, an obsessive/compulsive personality who has a powerful need to succeed. The fact that he has chosen medicine as an occupation is highly significant to his future growth as a person and family member. For work is a major part of a man's life, forming the basis for income, prestige, self-image, and his place in society.

"A man's occupation places him within a particular socio-economic level and work world. It exerts a powerful influence upon the options available to him, the choices he makes among them, and his possibilities for advancement and satisfaction. His work world also influences the choices he makes in other spheres of his life. Occupation has important sources within the self and important consequences for the self. It is often the primary medium in which a young man's dreams for the future are defined, and the vehicle he uses to pursue those dreams. At best, his occupation permits the fulfillment of basic values and life goals. At worst, a man's work life over the years is oppressive and corrupting, and contributes to a growing alienation from self, work, and society."

To the type of personality that is drawn to a career in medicine add the consuming intensity of the training process that occurs during his critical early adult years when he should be, but isn't, free to develop emotional and social maturity—and you have the evolution of an individual who never learns to cope with his own or others' human frailties or to handle the give and take required in normal relationships.

According to Julie C. Donnelly, who wrote her Harvard University doctoral thesis on "The Intership Experience: Coping and Ego Development in Young Physicians," "During early adulthood critical aspects of both work and family are consolidated. Because of the saliency of these issues, development at this time of life is likely to be stressful no matter what the individual life circumstances. Certain demanding professions are known to present particularly great obstacles during young adulthood. Medicine appears to be among the most problematic of the professions. The length and strenuousness of the training process rarely leave a reserve of emotional or physical energy for . . . one's intimate relationships."

As pointed out by psychiatrist Dr. Myra Hatterer, "At a stage in one's development when the mature give and take and openness of adult life should be developing through exploration of one's feelings, the young physician is often most unable to give time to himself and his wife. . . . An awareness of the importance of this stage of one's life, not only for the development of a career, but also for the development of maturity and sexual and emotional intimacy, is essential."

Thus the doctor is often an undeveloped human being who is thrust into a position of power over the lives of others without the compassion, understanding, and self-awareness required to handle the role. Result? He becomes either a self-deluded tyrant who begins to believe his own publicity and issues edicts at home and in the office or an anxiety-ridden creature whose deep-seated doubts of his ability to measure up to his omniscient role result in his constantly dodging the stress of confrontations with his family.

Dr. George W. is a handsome man with distinguished touches of gray at the temples and an athletic physique that evokes memories of his days as a college football player. He is a successful surgeon, if success is measured by the adoration of patients. By professional standards of success—referrals from other doctors and peer respect—George has not achieved any great standing in his field. However, the con-

stant accolades from his patients nurture his ego to an in-
toxicating degree and as the years go on he invests more and
more of himself in these doctor-patient relationships.

His wife, Erin, has watched George's growing immersion
in his work with dismay, at first, then anger and resentment.
Erin and George met when he was interning at a large Midwestern urban hospital. She came from a family of business
people and was enchanted with the romantic image of the
healer and the entire medical mystique.

"When we first got married," said Erin, "I looked upon
the hospital with awe. That was where they did all those
marvelous things to save people that George used to tell
me about. Later along, as the years went on and we had the
children, I grew to hate the hospital. It was my enemy."
Erin is a shy, soft-spoken introspective woman whose
quiet personality is in sharp contrast to George's almost
bumptious arrogance. For someone filled with self-doubts
and questions about the fitness of things in the universe,
the arrant self-assurance that George exuded was a compelling magnet. Here was a man filled with certainty and
the absolute belief that he had all the answers. After they
were married, Erin began to discover that this supreme
ego of George's was a living thing that had to be fed and
nurtured constantly. When she met his mother, she knew
where it had all begun. George had two sisters, he was the
son, the embodiment of his mother's dreams; not only did
he fulfill her fantasies by being handsome and a good student, but he was a surgeon as well. George's mother plainly
adored him to the exclusion of her other children; everything he said or did was endowed with greatness. Within
seconds of seeing the mother and son together, Erin suspected she would have a problem.

But George assured her that all that adulation bored him
and he found it cloying, and in her naïveté, Erin believed
him. But as time went on, she realized that he needed that

ego gratification like he needed food. And she knew that she could never supply it.

But Erin was busy with her job in the museum, and George was only home every third night, so there wasn't much time for examinations of relationships. And then, when residency was completed, they decided it was time to have a family. George made his hospital affiliation, opened a practice, and they bought a modest house in a nice suburb. First came Glenn, then two years later, Lisa. While the children were small, George was building his practice and reputation, and Erin realized she could not expect him to be home as much as she would like. After all, she had seen her father build a business and remembered the time it took. But within five years, George was established, and nothing had changed. In fact, George was away from home more than ever, and life seemed to be a series of broken promises and lonely days and nights.

"You promised Glenn you'd positively be at his Little League game!" "You promised you'd help Lisa with her science project!" Erin, who used to enjoy gourmet cooking, gave it all up in disgust after a particularly special dinner was ruined because George forgot to come home. "Perhaps I wouldn't have minded so much if I really believed there was validity in George's explanations." But she began to feel that the dedication to his patients was more involved with his ego than their well-being. She knew his patients idolized him because they constantly told her so whenever she ran into one. "Ooh," the patient invariably gushed, "your husband is a god!" George became more and more insufferable and, worse, unreachable. Erin was constantly complaining and she began to detest the role he had driven her into—the nagging, carping wife. The soft, sweet, and trusting look that had always been such an attractive part of her mien was gone; in its place was the face of a sad, bitter woman. She tried to get George to talk about their deteriorating relationship and about the parental deprivation he was imposing upon the children, but to no avail. He always had to dash off to the hospital.

Until the evening of Open School Week, when Erin went to visit Glenn's new classroom teacher. "I'm sorry my husband couldn't be here," Erin started to say when she noted the teacher's surprised expression. "But I thought you were divorced or widowed," said the teacher. "Glenn's problems are so clearly those of a boy without a father."

Erin confronted George at eleven o'clock that night when he returned from the hospital, and she exploded in fury—highly uncharacteristic behavior for this shy and gentle person. The well-being and future of her child were at stake—and all her normal repressions vanished under the powerful impetus to protect her young. George was absolutely stunned by the violence of her reaction—but it was a release of all the slights, hurts, and resentments she had been harboring for all the years of their marriage. She accused him of abandoning his responsibilities as a father and husband—of deliberately choosing his patients and the hospital as the focus of his life in preference to that of his family and home. "You don't have to be there all the time. No other surgeons we know spend as much time at the hospital as you."

Erin screamed and harangued until suddenly she realized she could have been talking to the wall; George was just sitting there totally unperturbed.

"Are you through?" he asked quietly when Erin stopped. He then proceeded to state calmly that in his view he was an excellent parent who provided his family with all the possessions and luxuries they needed. As far as his relationship with Glenn, George pointed out that being a conscientious, successful member of the medical community provided his son with a role model that was in the finest American tradition. "I don't have to be here at all times. Bringing up the children is your job." And then he went on to accuse Erin of poor performance as a mother. According to George, any flaw in the children's behavior was attributable solely to her since "child-rearing is the woman's responsibility." He then stalked out and returned with a pill and a glass of water. "Take this," he said, "you're absolutely overwrought. I'm leaving for my office." And he did.

It took Erin a week to get over this brutal encounter. And the time was especially torturous because George handled the matter as though he was the injured party—and refused to talk to her at all. This silent treatment caused currents of strain in the house that made the children fearful. Glenn reacted by being aggressively offensive and boisterous, which prompted his father to chastise him continuously. And Lisa just stayed in her room as much as possible with the door closed. Finally, Erin could bear it no more.

One evening after George had furiously ordered Glenn to leave the dinner table because he had spoken to his father with disrespect, and Lisa sat at her place with tears coursing silently down her cheeks, Erin blocked George's exit as he was leaving for evening rounds. "This can't go on, George. We must go for some help." He regarded her coolly and said, "I agree help may be needed—but not by me. Obviously you're having a problem—then you go. I'll be happy to pay for a psychiatrist for you." And he walked out.

Erin nearly decided to ask for a divorce at that moment. But then a number of factors came into consideration. She still loved George, and what improvement would divorce offer the children? And then, he was so sure it was all her fault. Maybe it was; perhaps it was her problem alone after all. In effect, it was. Because a problem does not exist unless it is perceived as such. And in George's I-am-never-wrong world, where his self-image of the absolute was fostered by adoring patients, he was a perfect person. They listened to him and never questioned his judgment. The nurses and residents listened to him and never questioned his judgment. Ergo: He is wise, capable, and a leader among men. Obviously, a hysterical woman is no match for a man of his stature, and if there is any malfunction in the operation of the household, the fault is unquestionably hers.

Positive self-belief is awesome and intimidating to most people, but especially to Erin, whose basic insecurity was coupled with the sense of fairness that caused her to examine every aspect of an issue—a combination of qualities that virtually crippled her into inactivity. She was initially drawn to George because of his self-assurance, which she mistook for strength, but was frequently angered by his dogmatism while secretly envying it. Life is so simple when you deal only in absolutes, and George projected an unruffled calm that conveyed utter confidence. Erin had sought an unusual degree of protectiveness in her marital relationship—and heretofore she had found George's authoritarianism very satisfactory. Now she realized the dreadful cost she paid for this false security.

His ability to make firm, fast decisions was, as frequently is the case, based on a combination of conceit that blinded him to the possibility of error and narrow-mindedness that made him totally unaware of other people's sensitivities. Now when Erin needed understanding, there was no one to supply it. When she sought a supportive exchange of ideas about their children and their relationship, it was impossible because George did not regard her as his peer. He was not accustomed to holding discussions with subordinates; he made judgments, gave orders, and expected compliance. The pattern had been set in their marriage and the very aspects that Erin had at first found comforting she now found constricting. She had the sense to realize the hopelessness of ever getting George to see her point of view—or any other than his own. George's behavior and personality were, by now, carved in stone. When the full realization hit her, Erin went outside to her favorite sitting spot near the bird feeder and sobbed for over an hour. Then she quieted down and calmly went over the alternatives in her mind and came to a conclusion: She would go into therapy to help her find out what within her had drawn her to a personality like George's; why her needs compelled her to stay; and how could she live in peace with him now.

Today, still married after twenty-five years, Erin's therapy has taught her to be more accepting of George's absences and lack of involvement with her and their family; she has learned to understand him and to show her anger more often. But nothing can equip her to cope with the sense of despair and loneliness she feels in sharing her life with a husband who considers her secondary in his life.

The most often heard plaint in letters received from doctors' wives is their resentment that their husbands put the needs of patients first, ahead of home and family, much as the wives of corporate executives or lawyers complain that their husbands' priorities are business first and family second. But the difference here is the doctor's wife cannot even enjoy the luxury of pure anger and resentment, because these feelings must be tempered by guilt, for how can she in good conscience expect any other behavior? If her husband is true to his oath and calling and performs as she should want him to—dedicating himself to the health, well-being, and survival of his patients—then priorities dictate that family and home must be his secondary, not primary, consideration. She may know this to be true, but the letters indicate a sense of abandonment and rejection that they, like Erin, have had to come to terms with but never truly accept.

"My husband's patients always come first and still do! I raised three children with only his financial help," writes a Pittsburgh doctor's wife.

Although 53 percent of the women surveyed by *Medical/Mrs.* claimed to have anticipated them, the time and energy demands of the medical profession were seen as taking a tremendous toll on a doctor's family. "No family life," wrote a Florida wife of eighteen years. "No time for wife and kids; keeps on getting worse. I raise the children all by myself. I will probably leave him one day." Many of the women resent their husband's failure to accommodate to the family. "He never asks if his schedule conflicts with mine or the family's. We have to arrange our schedule around him if we want him present," said one wife of thirty-one years.

One of my saddest letters came from a New Jersey physician's wife. "My husband was the son of a doctor, receiving a distorted image of what it meant to be a doctor. As he has grown older the image of what a doctor should be has become more and more distorted. He never thought of himself as a father or a member of the human race but only as 'The Doctor.' My life is hell on earth. I am caught in a financial bind that can't be resolved. I am tortured by my husband. My problem began when I first married and was too naïve to realize what was going on. It's too late now to help him or myself." And to the question "Would you encourage your daughter to marry a doctor?" she answered in large underscored letters "NEVER!"

A pediatrician's wife was particularly resentful since she sees her husband as expending all his energies and emotions on other people's children rather than theirs. "My husband is a pediatrician, the only one in town," writes a Florida woman. "We have three children, ages seven, five, and six months. The only problem is getting his expert opinion regarding raising kids he rarely sees (his own). He is so tired that he hates to discipline our children, who he may see for an hour. I'm left to raise the family, and to provide a buffer from the outside world when he comes home. I *often* feel there's none of me left and what is left is boring." As to the answer to the question "Would you encourage your daughter to marry a doctor?" she answers emphatically, "I'm not going to even encourage her to marry!"

Another woman from New Jersey says bitterly, "He led me to believe he loved children, but he never had any time for them. He always had time for weekly golf, fishing, and bowling for himself, but never shared any time with our children. He always expected to be waited on hand and foot and treats his wife like hired help, ordering, not asking."

A complaint that crops up again and again in correspondence and in the returned questionnaires is that "he orders us around" and brings the dictatorial operating-room command tactics into the home.

> Doctors are used to being waited on and expect it at home. They expect home to be an escape from pressure. They expect the burden of a good marriage to be on the wife. They are selfish and insensitive. (Maine)

> My husband's fanatic ways, carryover from his profession, drive me and my daughter crazy. He is sensitive where his patients are concerned, but not for us. (Pennsylvania)

According to Dr. Daniel H. Labby, professor of psychiatry and medicine, University of Oregon Health Sciences Center, in an article in a special *Medical Economics* (1979) issue devoted to a survey of physicians' life-styles,

> There are many parallels between the way a doctor manages patients and the way he manages his children. He must retain reasonable control over his children while supporting in them a sense of autonomy, fulfilling their increasing need for freedom of choice.
>
> The doctor pays many pipers for his failure to be consistently available as a parent. Fatigue and impatience may result in impetuous and not always fair decision-making. Professional style often carries over into family style: He handles his children in the same assembly-line way he handles a crowded waiting room of patients—a quick review of the chart plus a cursory exam.

But children, like patients, believe they deserve undivided attention to their problems. If Dad the Doctor is always unavailable, the children have little opportunity to see Mother and Dad negotiating together and making policies about such things as allowances and general activities, little chance to see differences melded through the practice of the healing art of compromise.

A heavily outnumbered Mother may resort to dictatorial tactics that prevent children from becoming voting members in the family. Exquisitely aware that Father's reward for long hours and hard work is to return home late and grumpy, they may not be willing to follow his example. For the doctor's part, he may miss early signals of impending major problems, which with an absent parent are more liable to go underground.

The unfortunate tendency to bring home the imperious conduct of the hospital can cause tremendous pain, anguish, and often tragedy to the children of physicians.

Jeff is the son of an Arizona physician. Ten years ago, he was a carefree, outgoing typical seventies teenager whose life priorities were rock music, eating, and school. Early in life, Jeff learned that the way to handle his father was with a stream of "yessirs" and "nosirs." "You could never talk to him because you could tell he wasn't listening." He shrugged his shoulders. "I guess my stuff just isn't as important as the things he does all day. You know, people sick and dying and all that." Jeff was not a great student, a fact he knew displeased his father. "He wants me to be a hotshot straight A like he was. But I don't care like I guess he did." Jeff's father cared a great deal about scholastic achievement and polite, circumspect behavior and neatness. An ex-navy man, the doctor had never forgotten his seagoing days and still sported the close-cropped crewcut of those early years. He could not understand his son's easy ways and casual dress, which he saw as evidence of weakness and moral deterioration. "Sure, I love my dad," says Jeff. "He's a good doctor—

that's what his patients say—and I know he does his best for them. But what does that do for us? I wish he were home more." Yet when his father was home, Jeff was learning to avoid him as much as possible because contact invariably led to confrontation. It would be a lecture on lateness to the dinner table, or a tight-lipped tongue-lashing about poor grades and the prospects of the dismal future that Jeff's lack of scholastic achievement promised. Surrounded all day by high adulation from patients, Jeff's father came home with the expectation that the same adoring, respectful attitude would be there waiting for him. What he didn't realize was that the family needed that kind of approval and approbation from him more than he needed it from them. As their confidence became eroded by his obvious lack of esteem, his wife and children became less secure, less happy. They needed his support and all they received was his scorn.

By the time Jeff was sixteen, the relationship between him and his father had deteriorated into open warfare. The father's hostility was exacerbated by his wife's constantly siding with Jeff. Her attempts to explain that today's teen-agers are different from the economically and sociologically pressured young of the 1940s, that wearing jeans and long hair did not portend the collapse of civilization, were totally unacceptable. He did not agree, he did not approve, and as he was the lord and master of the home, his orders were to be obeyed without question, as they were at the hospital. Unfortunately, he saw his home as merely an extension of his practice and would simply brook no challenge to his authority.

Jeff began to find home so unpleasant that he developed a life away from the house, leaning heavily on playing his guitar for friends and in school, first as a means of escape and then pleasure. As his skill with the instrument grew, it became apparent that here was an area in which he could truly excel. He began to study music intensively and then moved slowly into composing. As he became a musician,

Jeff started to develop a new secure identity and he began to dress the part. He let his hair grow until it was shoulder length. To his jeans and workshirt he added a red headband. But at home, when he heard his father, he removed the red headband before coming downstairs. As it was, the sight of the long hair was enough to send the doctor into a state of irritation and stifled fury. Jeff never talked to his father about his musical achievements, which were becoming considerable, because the doctor regarded Jeff's guitar as a toy and his music as an impractical time-waster that merely served to provide further distraction from his schoolwork.

In fact, Jeff never talked to his father at all.

One day, he was approached by members of a semi-professional rock group who had heard him perform at a school function and they invited him to join them. Jeff was ecstatic. It was the first time in his life that he had ever achieved recognition, admiration, and approval due solely to his own drive and talent. These jobs would not interfere with school since performances were on weekends. And he would be paid!

Jeff fairly flew home to tell his mother and sister, both admirers and supporters. He threw open the front door and came face to face with his father, who had just walked in. The doctor took one look at the long hair, which looked somewhat wild from Jeff's open-top ride home, topped by the red headband—and he exploded.

"You look like an idiot. Like a hippie freak. That's it—that long hair has got to go." And he reached in his medical bag and took out a scissors. "If you won't get it cut—I'll do it for you!" He grabbed Jeff, who started to yell and pull away. His mother and sister heard the racket and came running in. The doctor was absolutely ferocious and before anyone could stop him had hacked off one side of Jeff's hair. His sister started to cry and ran upstairs. His mother began screaming, "Stop it! Stop it!" But there was no stopping him. All the anger at what he perceived as rebuffs to his authority, all the resentment toward this son who seemed to get more sympathy and love from his wife than he, all the fury at this boy who had undermined his role as paterfamilias and proved him a failure as a father, erupted into a powerful attack he could not control. No matter how much Jeff tried to escape, no matter how much his mother tried to intervene, nothing could break the doctor's hold on his son. In a few minutes, Jeff's hair was laying in bunches on the hall floor. When he finally got free, Jeff looked at his father with burning hatred. "That's the only solution you know, you surgeon bastard—to cut!" He turned around and ran out of the house. And he never returned.

For many offspring of physicians, childhood is a bitter experience that marks them indelibly. "I hate it; I hate it," said one doctor's child. "He's never home. He never has time for us. He takes care of everyone but his own children. I wish my father was a lawyer, a businessman—anything but a doctor." In a *Medical/Mrs.* article called "Dad's a Doctor, Big Deal! What the Children Think," the most common complaint voiced was simply, "I never see him."

Judy, a suburban New Yorker in her teens, was more than willing to tell of her frustration with a father who was hardly around, and too tired for her and her sister when he was. Judy readily credits a turn to militant feminism to her home life. "As much as his behavior bothered me," she says, "I resented what it did to my mother even more. She was considered queen of the community. The doctor's wife. The woman who married well and had everything she could possibly want. Everything, that is, except her husband when she needed him."

The effect of paternal treatment that they see as ranging from opprobrious to oppressing has a dually devastating effect on daughters. Not only does the female child suffer from the absence of a doting daddy, but, as a woman, she identifies with the deprivations imposed upon her mother.

"I hated what he did to my mother," said one young adult daughter of a Michigan physician. "My vision of their life was that he was always wrong and she was right: He would never give an inch on anything. They fought so much—I seemed to spend my young life trying to keep them together. I should have spent more time on myself instead of them. There just seemed to be no pleasing him."

The desire for parental approval is a basic universal drive. The parents who structure expectation from their offspring at realistic levels, tailored to the ability of the individual child rather than the parents' own egoistic fulfillment needs, are sure to create a happy home environment. But this is fantasy in a medical family where we are dealing with a doctor-father who has achieved an elevated, respected position due to scholastic ability and intense drive, often the result of pressures imposed upon him by his own parents. He sees himself mirrored in the eyes of society as a super being. How can he allow his children, his derivatives, to be anything but achievers? A display of less than outstanding performance is a reflection on him . . . his genes, his ability as a father. The children know it, and their constant quest for their doctor-father's approval can lead to disastrous results.

Sharon is an extremely bright and articulate young woman of twenty-five. She grew up in a suburb of Chicago with all the accoutrements of affluence befitting the family of a successful physician. "We had expensive clothes, went to expensive schools and on expensive vacations. Sure I enjoyed all that—but I would have at any time gladly traded it for a loving, caring father."

As long as she could remember, Sharon was aware of her father exerting an autocratic effect on the family. And of everyone striving to please him. Her mother seemed to fear his ire and was totally submissive. Yet from time to time she would explode and the scene would frighten Sharon. The consequences were even more detestable; her father would punish her mother by not talking to her for days and the tone of the household became painfully strained, especially for a sensitive child who felt in some ways it was her fault.

And then when he was ready, even though he may have been wrong, he would "forgive" and resume household relations as though nothing had happened. Sharon's relief on those many occasions was always overwhelming. "He set it up that way," says Sharon now. "Even though he had been wildly wrong, I was so happy when he broke down that awful silence barrier that I was *grateful* to him for bestowing forgiveness upon us. It was sick!"

Sharon was the first born and always felt that she had failed her father by being a girl. He was a tall, powerfully built man who had followed the basic American dream guideline rules: study hard, be a dutiful son, serve your country (he had been an army captain in World War II), work hard, serve your profession, and produce an upstanding family to maintain this splendid tradition. The system had worked well for him and he saw absolutely no reason to alter it one iota. Totally insulated from the usual erosions of life, such as performance failures and financial difficulties, and blessed with tunnel vision that eliminated his awareness of any unpleasantnesses endured by real folks living in changing times, he was utterly smug.

Sharon saw her father as a hard-to-reach man. "Now I realize that he doesn't know how to deal with people on anything but a patient-physician level. That means putting on that fake bedside bonhomie, you know: 'Well, how's the leg today—ready to dance with me?' And all that superficial encouragement shit that he thinks patients want to hear. They probably do—but I don't."

His whole personality and behavior at home were carryovers from hospital and office where he saw himself as a father figure—giving firm advice, stern instructions, smiling reassurances, and being responded to with obedience, respect, and gratitude. He saw life in the most simplistic terms; people had problems, he had cures. As explained in the chapter "The Myth of Curing" from *The Medical Merry-Go-Round*, "Patients put pressures on their doctors to be all-knowing and invulnerable. Because psychological and social forces push in the same direction, doctors are drawn into the trap of taking credit for curing the patient. No matter what illness a patient had, no matter how much or how little the doctor's actions actually affected the outcome, the physician accepts the mantle of expert curer."

Sharon's father was very comfortable with that mantle. At no time was he aware of the real feelings of people he dealt with; it just wasn't within his area of understanding, and in his mind was unimportant to professional performance. That stuff was strictly for the psychiatrists, whom he regarded with contempt.

As Sharon grew older, she tried to touch him in some way. He was always working at the hospital, in his office. And patients were always given the home number and encouraged to call—which meant constant intrusions into their home life. She tried to please him, and looked forward to the rare moments they had together with no one else around. But she always came away from these encounters with a sense of disquiet and failure. It wasn't her daddy she talked to, it was a doctor person who heard her without listening and had never learned to invest anything of himself in relationships. When she tried to discuss matters that affected her deeply, he responded with either judgments or a bedside-manner banter that instantly transformed her concerns into trivialities. She sought understanding and was met with banality.

Obviously his work was the all-important element of his life to him. Thus the best way to please him, she reasoned, would be to enter his work world. So one day Sharon decided she, too, would be a doctor and then he would be proud of her. But it would be a secret, special "gift" she was preparing for him that no one must know about until the time of presentation. When Sharon entered high school, she checked the requirements of Brown University, her father's alma mater, and structured her school program to the goal of acceptance with a heavy stress on science courses. She liked science but truly loved dramatics. Since the highest possible scholastic rating was demanded for acceptance into the premed program at Brown University, which meant total commitment to study, Sharon turned down the coveted role of Annie Sullivan in *The Miracle Worker*, the play that was to be the main dramatic event of the school year. She was heartsick because she longed to play the part, but the amount of time required for rehearsals would be an impossible infringement on the program of study she had mapped out for herself. During the next three years, Sharon drove herself to get straight A's. The more she heard of the competition for acceptance by the college and medical school of her choice, the harder she worked. All outside activities were abandoned; her sights were set and she was determined to reach her goal. Sometimes, when particularly weary and lonely, she would envision the smile of pride on her father's face when she presented him with that great achievement, acceptance into the premed program, and it all seemed worth it. At no time did she stop to consider how she would like being a doctor. Not a moment's thought was given to the usual evaluation factors when deciding upon a life career. Sharon never envisioned herself doctoring; she saw herself only as a doctor, a peer and colleague of her father's. When college application time came, Sharon had amassed an impressive scholastic and science achievement record. Not only was she accepted by Brown University, but she was invited to join their special six-year premed right-through-medical-school program in which you enter as a college freshman and depart as a full-fledged physician. It was indeed an honor and a tribute to her talent and effort. Sharon was numb with excitement. The letter had arrived on the morning of April 15—and she knew her father would not be home until late that night. After all those years of work and planning, she just couldn't hold out any longer, so she committed an unprecedented act: She phoned her father's office and asked for a few moments of his time. When she entered his office, he greeted her with the indulgent-father phoniness she used to feel he picked up from Robert Young's *Father Knows Best* TV show. "To what do I owe the pleasure of this rare visit? Need some money for a new dress?" But this time, Sharon felt he could no longer put her off with that condescending "how's my cute but helpless little girl" routine. She was about to show him she could now meet him on his own turf.

"Daddy, I've been accepted by Brown's premed program. I'm going to be a doctor!"

The look on his face was one of total surprise, then disbelief, and then irritation. Sharon, who was expecting anything but this reaction, was shocked. In her fantasies about this moment, he came toward her with outstretched arms and a face beaming with paternal pride. He might even then take her around the office, with his arm around her shoulders, presenting her to all the nurses and other physicians in the office with the wonderful news, "My daughter is going to be a doctor."

She was stupefied. "But aren't you pleased? I did it for you!"

"For me?" he said with apparent annoyance. "What on earth did you do that for? You know what I think of women doctors!"

The insensitivity displayed by doctors is frequently staggering. Everyone has a story about an encounter with a doctor when bad news was delivered to frightened, vulnerable people in a sledgehammer fashion that bordered on brutality. I had a doctor tell me after the failure of vascular surgery he had performed on a member of my family: "He [the patient] contracted a severe infection during surgery—it happens. It's near a crucial artery, and we can't identify the bacteria yet. If the infection does not kill him within the next three days, I'll probably have to amputate his leg next week." This was information for which I was totally unprepared, and it was delivered in a curt, blunt manner that was, in effect, sadistic. There is no doubt that doctors must, of necessity, become somewhat desensitized to pain and death, for if they let the sufferings of every patient reach them, they would ultimately destroy themselves and become ineffective. But compassion and an awareness of the sensitivities of others would make them better doctors as well as better people, husbands, and parents. Yet, nothing in their training prepares them to deal with emotions, only bodies. No patient ever dares to attack them for callousness or cruelty in their dealings with feelings for fear of antagonizing them—and thus jeopardizing the chances of getting the doctors' best efforts.

I can remember my husband berating me once for writing a stinging rebuke to his doctor for what I considered inhuman behavior toward our family in not informing us of procedures. "You'll get him mad at me," my husband had said. When he thinks of his fears now, they seem foolish. But while a patient is under the care of a doctor, his whole concern is the physician's performance, and since attitude does have a vital part in one's working achievements, it is not unreasonable to want the doctor to like you.

That kind of patient-and-family apprehension coupled with the general awe with which he is regarded insulates the doctor from the truth about what a bastard he really is, when he is. This false perception of his character as seen through the never critical eyes of his patients makes him tough to live with indeed.

"Living with a man who presents an image to his patients and staff of 'the doctor,' but is at home unable to communicate—or unwilling, as it implies an equality in a relationship that his arrogance does not allow—has been very difficult," wrote a twenty-two-years-married New Jersey doctor's wife to *Medical/Mrs.* magazine. "He is a very controlling person, of the food that is to be served, the house money, of course, and my time is monitored as well, as any life I have of my own is threatening to him."

Why does a woman stay with such a man? Because she must be a passive, dependent person who seeks to be controlled and chooses a life of subordination. In many of these situations, the real victims are the children, who have had no say in the dominant-submissive structure their parents established to suit their own neurotic needs.

Sylvia and Daniel had a relationship that was painful to witness. Daniel, a hematologist in a big-city hospital, was an arrogant, pompous man who believed implicitly in his own opinions in human as well as medical matters. The product of a manipulative mother who convinced him of his superiority, he inflicted his domination upon Sylvia, who bent with his wishes and withered under his and his mother's criticism.

Daniel exercised full control at home over his wife's and children's activities. Sylvia was compliant, of course, but their daughter, Wendy, was not. Daniel was basically a fool whose academic success had led him to conclude that he had the ability to make wise decisions in all aspects of life . . . his and everyone else's. He tyrannized the family with a series of rules—how many hours were to be spent on homework, curfews—and even involved himself in the selection of his children's friends and extracurricular activities.

Wendy was a very bright girl who loved literature, art,

and was fascinated with esoteric aspects of philosophy. At age fifteen she was intellectually restless and wanted the freedom to explore every area. But her father's controlling interference prevented her from participating in any pursuit of which he did not approve. She felt stifled and suffocated and resented her mother's ineffectual role in her life.

One day Wendy went to an interschool meeting that brought her into contact with youngsters of a neighboring community, and she met two girls with whom she became "instant friends." Valerie was a sensible, strong-minded girl who was alternately angry, happy, rebellious, and spirited. Mary was a soft-spoken, somewhat lost adolescent whose gentle demeanor masked an inner discontent and a hunger to find some self-identity. Both girls came to visit and sleep over and to be submitted for Daniel's approval. He liked Mary because she was, on the surface, a compliant, respectful young lady who seemed to present no threat to his authority. But he did not trust Valerie because she was, in his eyes, a bad "hippie" influence on Wendy, and he tried to block the friendship.

Wendy had been chafing under her father's restrictive interference and she kept trying to assert her independence. One Saturday, she took the unprecedented step of taking the train herself and going to visit Valerie. Pleased with her accomplishment, she phoned home to merely advise them of her whereabouts. To her disgust, Daniel upbraided her fiercely for going without permission. "For God's sake— I'm fifteen. Why can't I go to visit my friend?" But in Daniel's moral code, any independent action undermined his authority, and he and Sylvia drove to Valerie's house immediately to take Wendy home. The dignity of an adolescent is a very delicate object, and the mortification Wendy felt at being reprimanded in this fashion before Valerie and Valerie's family was deeply wounding. The incident marked a turning point in Wendy's attitude toward her parents. Valerie, an eminently pragmatic person, had sympathized with her friend's chafing at the tight supervision of her life, but had encouraged Wendy to rebel in steps and to take a stand on important issues only, which Wendy had done. However, this humiliation removed all restraints, and now Wendy was angry and vindictive. She saw her father as a mindless tyrant who cared only for his own ego position, and her mother as a pitiful, spineless victim whose fears and weaknesses prevented her from giving Wendy any support or understanding. So Wendy proceeded to wound her father in the most overt ways possible.

Daniel, who saw Valerie as the damaging influence on his daughter, had encouraged Wendy's friendship with Mary. Always "the brilliant doctor" with the resultant distorted view of his abilities, Daniel never had the desire to develop an understanding of human behavior, which requires an ability to listen, observe, relate, and deduce. Guided by his dwarfed perceptions, Daniel saw Mary as safe. She was the daughter of a doctor, thus making her more respectable. (Valerie's parents were "creative" advertising executives— highly irresponsible in Daniel's view.) Also, she was quiet and shy, which to him bespoke a proper gentlewoman. If he had any insight at all, or if he had made the effort to tune into the times, he would have recognized that Mary's charming hurt-doe look was evidence of a child in pain. Mary, too, suffered from the repressions of a doctor-father, and had found her escape in drugs and gurus. She was a pot smoker who sought metaphysical solace from a succession of Eastern religions. Wendy, now furious and provoked, saw these routes as the perfect method of revenge and also personal fulfillment for her. She joined a guru's sect and became deeply involved in his Eastern teachings and religion. Her total immersion in the movement was evidenced by the saris she now wore. Her parents were stunned, and Daniel was unable to cope with this conversion since it presented elements he had never encountered. Wendy was now a proper, devout young woman who followed the precepts of a holy man. She was moral, decorous, and in no way could he fault her behavior.

Years later when Wendy graduated from Stanford University, Daniel and Sylvia sat in the audience, his pride mitigated by the shame he felt in front of the other parents when his daughter walked up to the platform to get her diploma wearing a colorful sari under the academic gown and accepting her diploma in the name of Ashanti, the guru-bestowed name by which she now chose to be known. Daniel knew he had lost all control over his daughter. Sylvia knew that she had lost all the pleasures of intimacy and companionship that are the priceless attributes of a good mother-daughter relationship. Unfortunately neither Daniel nor Sylvia ever understood why or how it had happened.

V

Doctors' Sex Problems: Inhibited, Inexperienced, Ignorant

It was a twentieth anniversary party and the gifts were being opened amid much banter and hilarity. The guest of honor came to an odd-shaped package that turned out to contain an elaborate screwdriver. Tucked in was a card which read "Happy Anniversary." The hostess whispered to her: "How much do you want to bet John makes some double-entendre remark?" Sure enough, as though on cue, Dr. John Bohlen guffawed and said with a leer "Screwdriver! I guess when you're married twenty years you need all the help you can get!"

Having led a cloistered academic existence in the early years when they should have been coming to terms with their own sexuality, doctors are uncomfortable with the workings of the libido and treat the subject of sex like oafish, inexperienced adolescents—with leers and snickers. Professionally, their attitude is frequently archaic.

In his article "The Physician as a Marriage Counselor," which appeared in *The Family Coordinator*, Dr. Joseph B. Trainer points out that doctors do fine with diseases of the genitalia and can give advice in a clear, straightforward manner with no trace of embarrassment. They will also do fine with maritally blessed pregnancy. But "any stage of the proceedings that introduces the hint of a purely sexual problem and the doctor shunts it off. . . ." It is a remarkable physician indeed who can discuss sex as fun with his patient, and do so in both a detached and relaxed manner. He seems peculiarly unable to manufacture the climate of ease and confidence which allows the patient to bring out her own uncertainties, anxieties, and fears.

"There are some glimmers of satisfaction for those of us in medicine who are interested in this field. One study, done about ten years ago, showed that the higher the professional status of the doctor (in the eyes of his colleagues) the more likely was he to adequately handle sexual and marital problems. Additionally, this defect is being realized in medical schools throughout the country and curricular changes are taking place to make the doctor more competent and more comfortable in sexual and marital counseling.

"Cecil's *Textbook of Medicine*—one of the great standbys of medical education—reflects these changes:

> Many areas of human functioning are overlooked in the course of ordinary medical study.
>
> The practicing physician often has little experience in areas involving a discussion of the sexual life of a patient.
>
> The majority of persons view the physician as one of the few people, perhaps the only person, with whom they may discuss, and are capable of discussing, their sexual functioning."

As reported in an article in *Playboy* called "Where Sex Is Concerned the Doctor Is Out" by Morton Hunt, not only are doctors not taught anything about sex in medical school, but a recent survey shows that today's medical students, like those who went before them, have distinctly less sexual experience than other college graduates of their age.

Many doctors-to-be simply are more misinformed and un-
informed than most of the world supposes. . . . Not only
wasn't your doctor taught anything about sex in medical
school, he probably didn't learn much about it through
personal experience, for during the years of training, medical students lead very restricted sex lives; medical school
leaves almost no time for the pursuit of personal relationships or pleasure. . . . Even more serious, studies made of
medical students in the sixties and early seventies report
that most of them are obsessive-compulsive personalities—
hardworking, precise, perfectionist, and self-controlled.
All of which is essential to anyone trying to get through
medical school; but such a personality configuration also
tends to make one sexually rather inhibited, puritanical,
distant, and thoroughly uncomfortable when forced to
discuss sexual matters or to deal with sexually troubled
patients.

That is why so many doctors, even today, avoid asking
their patients about their sex lives when taking their
history as part of the diagnostic search for the root of some
malady. A study made a few years ago found that among
doctors who see patients in primary care, more than half
do not routinely ask them anything about their sex lives,
though it can be as clinically revealing as those matters
they do routinely ask about—appetite, digestion, elimi-
nation, and the like. The study also showed that doctors
who don't ask about sex are only half as likely to spot
sexual problems as those who do, for many patients can't
bring themselves to volunteer the information and need
to have it drawn out of them.

Doctors who do ask about sex are often so ill at ease
when they do so that their patients find it hard to open up
to them and try to get off the subject as fast as possible.
When a doctor asks, with an oafish bonhomie that hardly
conceals discomfort, "And how are things in the sex department?" you have to be uncommonly dull or thick-
skinned not to recognize that the hidden message is "I
really don't want to talk about this."

They don't want to talk about sex because they are unaware of and inexpert in even the basic physiological aspects of human sexuality. Dr. Harold Lief, professor of psychiatry at the University of Pennsylvania and *doyen* of medical school sex educators, is the codeveloper of the Sex Knowledge and Attitude Test (SKAT), now widely used in medical schools. Dr. Lief says that recent feedback from schools using SKAT shows that before taking a course in human sexuality, nearly 10 percent of today's medical students believe the condom is the most reliable means of birth control; 15 percent believe that masturbation can cause mental illness; 27 percent believe that very few married couples ever have oral sex; and about 40 percent believe that there are two physiologically distinct kinds of female orgasm, the clitoral and the vaginal.

Marriage to a man with this kind of attitude toward sex presents problems that many young brides are not always capable of handling. Ignorance and lack of experience is not a deterrent to the development of a compatible sexual relationship, it is merely a temporary obstacle that can be overcome with mutual cooperation. But when one of the couple (1) sees nothing wrong with his performance, (2) is too narcissistic to be concerned with pleasing his partner, (3) is too inhibited to experiment with different sexual techniques, then the possibility of working out a satisfactory and fulfilling sexual consociation is dim indeed. "I have found the sexuality of doctors bizarre," writes a young woman who had been living with a doctor for over a year. "There is a much different level of loving, caring, sensitivity, almost just flat out fucking rather than being allowed to get into any real areas of feeling."

The pattern starts early in medical school or residency where the demands, both physical and emotional, drive the doctor into a state of exhaustion so that he is frequently unwilling or unable to perform sexually, and certainly in no condition to indulge the romantic fantasies of his wife. The complete self-absorption demanded by his professional training pervades every aspect of his life and becomes the cornerstone of an attitude of total disinterest in pleasing anyone but himself. Sex becomes a perfunctory performance with his wife as a spectator/participant.

As the years pass, the escalating ego gratification derived from his profession contributes to the development of emotional myopia. If his wife complains about his lackluster lovemaking, he will place the blame on her. She demands too much. (Doesn't she realize he is justifiably weary from slaving to provide the elements of the good life for her?) She has no compassion and understanding. (Doesn't she see that he is emotionally drained from seven hours of emergency surgery in a struggle to save the life of a man suffering from kidney failure?) She doesn't do enough to stimulate him. (After all, they have been married a long time.) These are the words he may say, but even more damaging is the unsaid: "I never get complaints from the nurse or patient I had a fling with last week."

And, of course, he wouldn't. The reverence and idolization with which nurses and patients regard doctors makes any liaison between them a travesty on reality. The fact that the great man has deigned to sleep with them is sufficient reward; sexual satisfaction lies in the act itself and not the consummation. Thus he would have a totally false gauge of his effectiveness as a lover, and any complaints from his wife would be received with skepticism.

Kay and Paul were married when she was nineteen and he twenty-two, the year he entered medical school. Both were virgins. Although such a situation would be rare today, in the 1950s, when they were married, the mores of the times dictated premarital purity for brides and accepted chastity for men. Paul was a studious chap who had little time for socializing and absolutely no experience with

women. He was shy and inept with them, and avoided
parties or gatherings where his social inadequacy would be
exposed. Kay was a quiet but determined young woman who
decided early on that she would like to marry a doctor who
represented security, prestige, and affluence—all the elements she foresaw in her future. When she met Paul at a
friend's house, where he was visiting the friend's brother,
Kay decided he would be her husband. To Paul, this attention from a female was unprecedented and delightful. He
rapidly fell in love with Kay, and she with him, and they
were married.

Paul's years of pent-up desire were released in a year of
passionate lovemaking. His concept of sexual intercourse
was basic: when aroused, immediate penetration, orgasm
(his), and finished. If his wife received gratification during
this performance, fine. If not, better luck next time. Since
Kay never had the chance to achieve climax, they accepted
it as a given that orgasms were strictly for men only. The
fact that Paul was a physician and thus familiar with the
functioning of the body reinforced Kay's acceptance of their
unsatisfactory sex life. After all, Paul studied about glands
and organs and reproduction, and if this was sexual normalcy
according to his professional standards, then this must be it.
She was not unhappy, merely mystified about the ecstasy
of sexual fulfillment that she had read about.

Paul was moving ahead in his field; he was a brilliant
endocrinologist and became the chairman of the department in a major medical school. Highly regarded by his
peers and patients, Paul developed the smugness and paro-
chialism typical of a man who has never truly been challenged.

Then came the 1960s and the morality climate changed.
Someone suggested that a course on human sexuality be
introduced to the first-year medical school curriculum.
Masters and Johnson were making sex therapy a respectable
medical specialty; the American Medical Association itself

suggested that medical schools teach human sexuality. After all, sexual dysfunction is an important element to be considered in any diagnosis. But Paul, like most doctors, was ill at ease with sex and tended to skirt the issue with his patients. And when forcibly confronted with a sexual problem, he would contaminate his advice with his own moral values and ignorance. When an nonorgasmic woman complained, he assured her that this was a common female condition and her enjoyment should be derived from her husband's orgasm. As head of the department, he fought and won the battle against the introduction of a sex course as foolish frippery not germane to the purely medical goals of effecting cures and prolonging life.

Meanwhile Kay was expanding her horizons. Their children were in school, and she went back to college for a master's degree in education. Suddenly she met up with the sixties generation head on. One of her instructors was a young man whose psychology course she found fascinating. An excellent student, she began to meet him after class to discuss her research, and a strong mutual attraction developed. One evening she stopped by his apartment to drop off her final term paper and the inevitable occurred. This was Kay's first sexual encounter with a man other than her husband, and it was an incredible experience that bordered on an epiphany. He fondled her, caressed her, performed erotic acts of foreplay until she reached a pitch of excitement, at which point he penetrated, and they both achieved orgasm simultaneously. She went home that evening in a state of shock. Heretofore coitus had been a ho-hum act, an exercise she tolerated because it was something Paul obviously enjoyed and she found sometimes mildly pleasurable and often a chore. She had made the assumption that if in fact sex could be exciting for the woman as well as the man, then she must be deficient in some way since she had never achieved orgasm. The possibility that it was Paul's fault had never entered her mind. Now she realized that her husband's lack of interest in her sexual gratification had deprived her of years of pleasure, and she was suddenly furious.

But she had a major problem. She did not love her instructor, she loved Paul. How was she to explain to her husband that she knew she could achieve orgasm without informing him of her infidelity?

The next night Paul approached her in bed with the expectation that she would, as always, comply. To his surprise, she demurred and started to talk instead. She told him she had learned in one of her psychology courses (not too far from the truth) that sexual satisfaction for the female is as possible and important as for the male, and she wanted to reach the same apogee of ecstasy during intercourse as he. Paul's astonishment turned to irritation. "Psychologists! What do they know. They're subprofessional assholes who have tried to carve careers out of bullshit!" Then he proceeded to inform her that most women who claim to have achieved orgasm are just faking, putting on an act to please their husbands. That in the "normal" mounting position of male atop female it was difficult for the penis to make contact with the clitoris, and since clitoral stimulation was mandatory for orgasm, the chances of a woman's climaxing were remote. It was all very clinical and absolute. Stark naked, Paul delivered this lecture with the intransigence of a man whose word is never questioned, and then, looking down at his no-longer-erect penis, he said, "Oh, hell, let's go to sleep." And he turned over and did just that.

Kay lay next to him fuming, unable to reach him, unable to sleep, her thoughts ran from sadness for her lost years, horror at the realization of the damaging misinformation Paul had been dealing out to patients, and despair at the hope of ever communicating with him on this topic. How could she tell him that she was the case that disproved his theories?

She saw the young instructor the following week and

found herself looking forward to the meeting with an excitement she never recalled experiencing. Sex was wonderful again—he was creative and uninhibited and Kay was once again orgasmic.

A few evenings later as Paul and she were having pre-dinner cocktails, a relaxation-time luxury that Paul's schedule rarely allowed, Kay brought out a book on sex that she had found in the college library and asked Paul's opinions about certain passages. She read aloud the section on the variations in coital positions and then, as planned, asked casually, "Why don't we ever try other positions?" Paul was shocked. "Are you serious? Why, that's obscene. What are you reading that pornographic junk for?" He was plainly discomfited and would not continue the conversation.

Although they usually had sex on the average of twice a week, Paul didn't approach Kay for over a month. Of course Kay never thought of making the overture—that just wasn't their style. And when he did, Paul found he could not attain erection and was mortified. Obviously the questioning of his performance had thrown him. Nothing in Paul's life had prepared him for failure. He had excelled as a student, and now as a professional. All his relationships were on a patient-doctor level where he patted heads and received respect and gratitude. Or on a professor-student and doctor-nurse level where he ordered and they obeyed. Or on a doctor-doctor level where outward mutual respect is the name of the game. Socially, he was eminently acceptable everywhere as "the doctor." Suddenly that most basic area that lies at the core of every man was being challenged: his masculinity.

Paul had been perfectly contented with their marriage and sex life and rarely felt the need for extramarital activity. Of course, there were some isolated episodes over the years with nurses and patients, and never had there been a hint of dissatisfaction from any of these casual partners. As a matter of fact, they seemed flattered by his interest. But he did not consider these encounters as having any relation to his wife and family, whom he loved and enjoyed.

He regarded Kay as an excellent wife. The house was well run, the children were well behaved, the home was singularly free of strain. In fact, when he'd hear doctors complaining in the locker room about difficult children, demanding wives, and other family problems, he would feel fortunate. The marriage seemed to suit Kay's and his needs in an ideally symbiotic way and never before had there been even a suggestion of discontent. Now sex, of all things. What had gotten into her? It was undoubtedly all that psychology course nonsense. As an endocrinologist, Paul felt particularly qualified to deal with sexual dysfunction and was totally unaware that he had been dispensing advice based on personal morality rather than fact. Since he had no premarital sexual experience whatever other than masturbation, and was never given any reason to be other than pleased with his businesslike brand of marital and extra-marital sex, he considered any other behavior lewd and abnormal. Oral sex was disgusting, anal sex abnormal, and any other than the male dominant mounting position an aberration. That Kay could even suggest such a thing was shocking. But even more upsetting was the implicit inference that she found his sexual performance inadequate. During all the years of their marriage, she had never indicated any discontent and seemed a perfectly willing sex partner.

Paul now found that he regarded Kay differently, and he wondered if he really ever knew her. The thought that he might be at fault entered his mind fleetingly, but was rapidly discarded; the years of obeisance accorded him solidified the belief in his own absolute rightness. If there was any problem, it was Kay's, not his. Kay noticed the subtle change in Paul's attitude toward her and was disturbed. She realized she had opened a can of worms that threatened the stability of their marriage. Sex had never seemed important to her before; in fact, she used to wonder what all the fuss was about. But now that she knew, things could never be the same . . . or could they? Kay was an extremely pragmatic woman who knew what she wanted and was fully aware that one paid a price for everything. She loved her home and family, she reveled in her affluence and prestigious position in the community as "the doctor's wife," and she made her decision. Never again did she make any reference to their sexual relationship. Soon Paul forgot the whole episode and their sex life resumed its regular unspectacular course. And Kay continued her liaison with the young psychology professor until he took a job at a university in a distant city. Then Kay met a handsome English literature instructor who cochaired a campus committee with her. . . .

Not all women are capable or desirous of resolving sexual incompatibility problems in the way Kay did. One major factor here is that she learned the fault was not hers and thus did not batter her ego with self-reproach. Also, she was willing to separate out the sexual aspects of her marriage and be comfortable with an arrangement (albeit one that was arrived at unilaterally) whereby each partner would find sexual satisfaction in his/her own way. But what about the woman who feels the failure is hers since the great doctor cannot possibly be at fault?

Studies have indicated that many medical marriages where sexual dysfunction exists have a father-daughter aspect to the relationship that subjects the wife to extremely destructive pulls and pressures.

From his study of "Psychiatric Illness in the Physician's Wife," read to the American Psychiatric Association, Dr. James L. Evans reported these results:

"Informants described fourteen patients as having been very close to their fathers, and the therapists of twelve patients felt that a father-daughter relationship existed between patients and their husbands. In addition, there was a mean elevation of the MMPI hysteria scale and a history of relative sexual incompatibility in at least 75 percent of the cases. Marriage to an older man, whose vocation may have been unconsciously associated with omnipotent, understanding, protective attributes may be interpreted as an attempt by many of the patients to resolve persisting Oedipal conflicts. Illness developed when the equilibrium of the adjustment was disrupted by such reality factors as the increasing involvement of the doctor in his work, or a conflict between his personality characteristics and the idealized expectations of his wife."

Finally, should the doctor's wife feel she must get counseling to resolve her feelings of frustration and despair, where can she go? Psychiatrists are doctors, and a frequent fear expressed was that "doctors stick together." And male doctors usually do. Their arrogance, built upon years of uncontested performance, leads them to view all criticisms of physicians from the laity as unwarranted attacks stemming from either ignorance or neurosis. They view complaints from doctors' wives subjectively and deal out advice that is self-serving, placing all the onus for compromise in the wives' corner.

Here is a column in *Medical/Mrs.* magazine wherein psychiatrists Dr. Myra Hatterer and her husband Dr. Lawrence Hatterer fielded a question on what to do about dull and desultory sex between a doctor and his wife.

DR. LAWRENCE HATTERER REPLIES: There are basic factors that can explain a deteriorating sexual relationship between a doctor and his wife. The major one is a life that is unbalanced, favoring work and neglecting play. Some doctors unconsciously slip into giving excessive attention, energy and even love, to their patients/teaching/research, with little or none left for their own mates. At the end of an exhausting day, the doctor finds it difficult to relax into intimacy and then move on to lovemaking. Many wives complain that there is no preamble to sexual activity. But a man doesn't need as much romantic interaction to feel sexual; love and sex are sex are not necessarily synonymous in his background. He complains that his wife needs to be brought around and isn't spontaneous or abandoned enough. He has had to be close to people all day. Whether he likes it or not, his patients tell him the most intimate things in their lives. Some even seduce and cater to his ego at high levels. He wants the same or more at home. His wife, in turn, wants her share of this high level of attention that he has given others throughout the day. Instead—fatigue, detachment, irritability, and, for a few, the need to be alone, to engage in a sport or a mindless activity and an undemanding interaction, is most desired.

The other most common reason is boredom with the same sex-play script. The easy predictable route is taken. Repetitious sensual rituals are pursued because of habit and emotional safety. Unless a couple examines how dull each may find the other in and out of bed and makes a try for something new and exciting, the mind, eye, and heart may wander. Fantasy, or even a real someone else, replaces them and represents a serious threat to their love for each other. For those who don't have the energy or desire for outside pleasuring, work becomes the embodiment of a mistress.

Not only is there a lack of conscious attention to where, when, and how often the doctor sex-plays, but he and his wife do not easily talk about what has happened to that side of life. It seems to be one of the last subjects that is dealt with in depth, despite our current sexual revolution. Sex manuals, jokes, gossip, are exchanged but each person's ego seems too sensitive for the subject to be given its proper input. Postponement becomes the major mechanism used to deal with the disappointments in one's love life. Change after the years of neglect and repetition is not easy. Doctor and spouse tend to shy away from the challenge of upgrading and making their sensual lives more adventurous. Neither party is willing to make the aggressive plunge and, as a result, the old habitual and often dull ways hang on. Each wishes the other would take action.

The wives wish for more romance, a thoughtful expression, some extra time leading up to that orgasm. The husbands fantasize those wild, active, instant overtures of seduction and catering to their "macho" to get their motors running. Instead, each is mutually disappointed and sometimes wounded by the other's neglect. They respectively retreat to separate corners or to isolating fantasies. What could be isn't. The solution? Someone should take or make the first move!

DR. MYRA HATTERER REPLIES: Sexual intimacy, like intimacy in general, is a state of relatedness that develops over a period of time. It is a state of mutual trust and complete sharing, coupled with understanding of and respect for each other's, as well as one's own, needs and desires. It is an evolving process.

Early in a relationship intense sexual desires and strong love feelings are likely to be present, which often are enough to bring gratification to both partners. At other times they are so overwhelming to one that the other partner is dissatisfied. Gradually, as the rush dies down, the couple explores each other, adjusts to one another, and tries to develop a mutually satisfying relationship. Ideally, time is available for this to develop. But unfortunately, the young physician who is frequently a house officer early in his marriage, is often too drained physically or emotionally by his work to be a living and attentive spouse. He may even be unable to devote much thought to his own emotional evolution. At a stage in one's development when the mature give and take and openness of adult life should be developing through exploration of one's feelings, the young physician is often most unable to give time to himself and his wife. He is faced with life and death responsibilities at a time when his knowledge and experience are still limited. And these are frequently the only emotional concerns he is able to cope with.

The young wife is either out in the working world, meeting others and thus expanding, or at home nursing children. A form of sexual gratification and emotional feedback can be gotten from her role. Frequently she gives more thought to her needs and those of her children and husband than he does. As a result, such a couple may move through the early years of their marriage at very different rates, both sexually and emotionally. This would prevent intimacy.

An *awareness* of the importance of this stage of one's life, not only for the development of a career but also for the development of maturity and sexual and emotional intimacy, is essential. This may be the stage of marriage where the wife has to give more. At the time when so much of his existence is pressured, and he has so little control over his life, sharing, relaxing, and time for close fun activities alone, without small children, is crucial. Whenever possible they should have sex, in a comfortable, unpressured setting (without his feeling obligated because he was on call the previous two nights). This is not easy to find under the early conditions of marriage, unless it becomes a priority in one's life.

In summary, giving your emotional and sexual needs as much awareness as your need for career building is a primary step in the development of intimacy. Working through not only the strains of an early career but also of marriage *together* can do much to foster the sharing and openness and mutuality of later life.

Note how Dr. Lawrence Hatterer paints the sympathetic picture of the harassed, put-upon, exhausted doctor who comes home to a wife who "complains," "needs to be brought around," "wants her share of attention he has given others." Then observe the bilateral point of view of Dr. Myra Hatterer. She starts right off placing the responsibility equally upon both partners. "It is a state of mutual trust and complete sharing, coupled with understanding of and respect for each other's, as well as one's own, needs and desires."

When the question about difficulties experienced in

medical school marriages was posed to psychiatrist Dr. Harold Marcus, note the sexist slant to his analyses and advice:

> A young doctor in training is busy, but he is home, and although his wife cannot spend time with him, he is physically there. In her loneliness, she tends to look forward to after training with the unrealistic expectation that their relationship will then be better. But once he enters private practice, the separation becomes more intensified instead of less. Now he is involved with meetings, rounds, patients' needs that may keep him away from home perhaps every second night. She becomes frustrated, angry, and deeply resentful. As a result, she withdraws from him, withholding sex and then love. In the hospital he is treated as a god, but at home he is treated as a man by a wife who is cold and critical. As a result he becomes angry, and the marriage is in trouble. If she wants the marriage to work, she must make up her mind to deal with him in a noncritical way and to avoid confrontations and angers. Doctors' wives, more than any other group, must make independent lives for themselves. She must have her own interests, be it a career, or politics, or volunteer work, so that she is not totally dependent upon her husband to fulfill all her emotional needs.

As Dr. Marcus sees it, while the dedicated husband is out there devoting himself to curing the ills of mankind, his selfish wife sits at home fuming at his neglect of her needs and childishly punishes him by withdrawing much-needed sex and love. "If *she* wants the marriage to work, *she* must make up her mind to deal with him in a noncritical way." Why? Obviously the doctor occupies some divine position that exempts him from the barbs directed at ordinary mortal husbands, and all adjustments in cases of medical marital discord must be made strictly by the wife. With this kind of medical-community attitude toward criticism of their confreres, medical wives are justifiably loath to take their problems to psychiatrists. Why then could not a troubled doctor's wife go for therapy to a psychologist or psychoanalyst who is not an M.D.? Because she cannot trust them, having been brainwashed for years by her husband's and his colleagues' scorn of practitioners who do not possess the prized, respected M.D. degree!

In the 1979 *Medical Economics* magazine's special issue devoted to doctors' after-hours lives, which was in effect a self-portrait of the American doctor, 64 percent of the surveyed physicians who complained of marital problems identified "unsatisfactory sexual relationship" as a cause. The medical specialty that produced the most sexual dissatisfaction among its practitioners was psychiatry. When questioned as to the cause of their incompatibility, one psychiatrist answered, "Spouse constantly nagging and critical. No sex, she's anorgasmic and doesn't want it."

Characteristically, few of those surveyed and quoted assumed any responsibility for their wives' unhappiness or the unsatisfactory state of their marital sex lives. They choose to ignore the causes that may have to do with depletion of energies imposed by the intense emotional demands of their practices which result in a slap-dash lovemaking approach that merely fills their needs but offers none of the romantic interaction desired by their wives.

This combination of the doctor dumping sexual dysfunction problems on his wife and her blaming the entire medical profession, thus causing a prejudicial antagonism toward medical psychotherapy, can lead to disastrous results as shown in the case described by Masters and Johnson in *Human Sexual Inadequacy* paraphrased below:

> Dr. and Mrs. F. were both in their mid-forties and had been married for twenty-two years. They went to the Masters and Johnson Reproductive Biology Research Foundation to solve the problem of Mrs. F.'s "primary nonorgasmic status." Dr. F. was a physician with a de-

manding practice. Although he was sexually adequate, he
had gradually become less and less interested in their sex
life over their twenty-two years of marriage. Before marriage he had had a few casual sex encounters, but after
marriage he was so completely dedicated to his work that
he had little time to devote to marriage and family.

Mrs. F. had had intercourse twice before she got
married, each time without experiencing orgasm. After
marriage, she immersed herself in community activities,
principally to distract herself from the growing pain of
sexual frustration. She sought help during her marriage
from a variety of different therapists, but to no avail. No
one seemed able to give her the secret of orgasmic release.

Her frustrating experiences with the therapists combined with the minimal attention she was receiving from
her doctor-husband created a severe aversion in Mrs. F.
to all things authoritative, especially if they were associated with the medical world. She blamed the medical
profession for her sexual dysfunction.

When Dr. and Mrs. F. went to the founndation, she
had completely rejected Dr. F. both as a man and as a
husband. And she was sure that the Foundation, as a
medical authority, would take her husband's side in any
approach to therapy for her sexual dysfunction.

"During the intake interviews, she was barely civil,
lashing out at the medical profession in general and her
cotherapists in particular."

As treatment progressed, Mrs. F. began to relax somewhat and became encouraged to find that she was becoming more sexually responsive. But then on the eighth day,
she and her husband got into a serious quarrel, and she
ˇimmediately returned to her former state of sexual rigidity.
By the next day, she was in a state of despair and anger;
she felt her case was hopeless and that the Foundation
had failed her.

"Suspecting the motives of the cotherapists involved,
Mrs. F., in the bitterness of her disappointment, viciously
attacked them as charlatans and accused them of taking
sides with her husband in the therapeutic program."

The foundation therapists discharged Mr. and Mrs. F. immediately and the marriage ended in divorce.

There are many sexual problems that crop up in medical marriages that are not necessarily profession-related. However, the severity is exacerbated by factors that are uniquely inherent to doctors, by societal attitudes toward the medical profession, and by circumstances that play out in specific ways because the person involved is a physician.

Jenny was introduced to Dr. Steven Parker by mutual friends who felt that her sophisticated, outgoing personality would be the catalyst to bring Steven out of the introverted shell that had kept him a bachelor at the age of thirty-seven. And they were right. Steven took to Jenny at once and opened up to her in a way that no one who knew the good, kind sedate doctor could believe. Jenny was twenty-eight years old and had a good deal of social experience, including numerous sexual liaisons. She was charmed with Steven's obvious devotion and courtly manners. He had an established practice in a community where he was highly regarded by his peers and much adored by his patients. Jenny's mother considered Steven a marvelous "catch" and phoned Jenny daily to remind her that she wasn't getting any younger. Even without maternal prodding, Jenny had decided that the time to settle down was at hand, and when Steven asked her to marry him, she accepted. During their engagement, Steven made no sexual overtures to her; he made it plain that he was old-fashioned and regarded sexual intercourse as improper for them in any other than the marital bed. Jenny found this attitude somewhat Victorian and droll, but she accepted it as part of the prim façade that she suspected masked a passionate nature that would be released when restrictions were lifted. They were married amid much feting and celebrating and sailed off on a honeymoon.

When they returned, the newlyweds were invited to

friends' for dinner. The hostess came out to greet Jenny while her husband was pulling Steven toward the bar. "I feel rotten, Jenny, I didn't buy your wedding gift yet!" Jenny looked at her friend silently for a moment and then said, "Wait."

What Jenny discovered on their wedding night was that she was right about the ferocity of Steven's suddenly released passion. What she hadn't predicted was the rapid-fire brand of coitus he considered sex. She was shocked that a man of thirty-seven, a physician, understood nothing of the love, affection, and touching she enjoyed and expected. Entry and ejaculation took place with speed and dispatch, and that was that. When she tried to talk about it, Steven became flustered and embarrassed and was unable to continue the conversation. She thought she would give him a few days to calm down, but became so incensed at his sexual treatment of her that she erupted and lashed out at him with accusations of selfishness, insensitivity, and boorishness. Very much in love with Jenny and almost pathetically eager to please her, Steven was bewildered by her reaction. He had enjoyed sexual relations with many women; it was always like this. What had he done wrong to upset her? Plainly uncomfortable under Jenny's questioning, Steven finally described his sex history. He had attended medical school in Scotland, where he had his first sexual experience with a prostitute, whom he continued to see on a fairly steady basis. He was expected to complete the act as quickly as possible; the faster he ejaculated the more he pleased her. After all, her business was based on quantity, not quality. Then he met a young local woman who was flattered by the attentions of the young American doctor. She was awed and adoring and eagerly compliant with his desire for sex. Conditions were less convenient than his previous experience since they had to use whatever out-of-the-way spots they could find or sometimes the backseat of his friend's borrowed car. Always it was a nervous, hurried affair with the constant fear of discovery. As a result, speed and rapid ejaculation was the preference of both partners and no concern for pleasuring the woman was even considered.

Steven's sexual behavior was conditioned by these experiences. As he saw it, fast was good because that's what the ladies seemed to want. When he returned to the United States, he was a doctor with all the prestige and honor the title conferred. From then on, his sexual relations with nurses, sometimes patients, followed the same pattern of performance and he never had a single complaint. Who would criticize the wonderful doctor? Sex play, mutual caressing, displays of affection and pleasing the woman were totally alien to him. In fact, he considered that sort of activity as mildly disgusting. He actually believed that sexual gratification was a male province and that women were merely passive participants. Jenny tried to explain her needs and feelings, but she could not reach him. The idea was abhorrent to him and he could not believe that Jenny's emotions were universal. The marriage was annulled three months later.

The key to solving any marital problem is, of course, communication between the partners. A free exchange of "I really hate that," "I know I'm wrong but help me cope with my anger," "I'm really unhappy because you've hurt me deeply"—an open discussion of each one's feelings about the other's behavior is the procedure prescribed by all marriage counselors for working out what bothers and eventually festers in a relationship.

The current "Me Generation" has taken to "communicating" and full disclosure with an enthusiasm that borders on obsession. "How I feel about myself and you and why" are discussed socially in torturous depth with a degree of intimate detail that one used to be unable to reveal even to oneself. Those of us who are products of earlier generations are untrained in the techniques of introspection and merciless self-evaluation. And even if we could learn to master the method, we have been schooled to restrain public airing and sharing of private feelings. Given these instilled inhibitions, the difficulty of communicating one's innermost emotions to even a husband or wife is monumental.

Then consider what position sex has been assigned in a woman's growth and development. During her formative years, she is given to believe that romance and love are proper feminine interests but sex is for men and boys only. The "good girl" façade must be maintained, and seeking— and worse, enjoying—sex is for "bad girls." A young woman who evidenced pleasure from sex was apt to be suspected as wanton. I know a man who distrusted his wife and sought fruitlessly for signs of infidelity for the fifty-seven years of their marriage because she responded to him with pleasure on their wedding night.

Add to this his-and-her sexuality hodgepodge the myth that all males are blessed with the instinctual ability to star in the sex act and you have a major obstruction to the development of connubial compatibility.

Again, according to Masters and Johnson:

> The most unfortunate misconception our culture has assigned to sexual functioning is the assumption, by both men and women, that men by divine guidance and infallible instinct are able to discern exactly what a woman wants sexually and when she wants it. Probably this fallacy has interfered with natural sexual interaction as much as any other single factor. The second most frequently encountered sexual fallacy, and therefore constant deterrent to effective sexual expression, is the assumption, again by both men and women, that sexual expertise is the man's responsibility. In truth, no woman can know what type of sexual approach she will respond to at any given opportunity until faced with absence of a particularly desired stimulative factor. How can a woman possibly expect any man to anticipate her sexual pleasure when she cannot ac-

complish this fact with consistency herself? How can any man presume himself an expert in female sexual response under these circumstances?

Spontaneous sexual expression which answers the demands to be sexually needed and gives freedom for comparable male and female interaction is universally the most stimulating of circumstances. Here the signal systems lead each partner toward and into the specifics that are desirable at a particular time. It is development of signal systems competent to deal with the response requirements (communication) toward which cotherapists gradually direct the marital unit.

And here we come back to that critical word "communication," without which no reconciliation of problems can be achieved. Burdened with the societal strictures on her enjoying sex, how can she be shameless enough to complain to her husband about not deriving pleasure from their sex life? Deterred by the psychosocial training that frowns on divulging intimate feelings, how can she feel free to talk to her husband about effecting changes in their sex habits? And if she finally overcomes all these hurdles, how can she communicate with a man whose idea of relating to people is listening to their complaints and prescribing instant solutions, issuing orders which are obeyed unquestioningly, a man whose vision of himself is the reverentially heeded hero who never suffers criticism? He is the doctor. If she has a problem with their sex life, she must find her own solution.

VI

Adultery: His and Hers

How would you feel if your husband spent his days and nights among unclad and semiclad doting women, surrounded by adoring young nurses, in a facility of wall-to-wall beds?

It's a setup for adultery. The situation is so conducive that it would be surprising if doctors did not have affairs, and they do, according to the flow of letters received by *Medical/Mrs.* from doctors' wives:

> Was there, is there, a doctor who can remain faithful when he is treated like Adonis by his nurses and patients? (New Hampshire)

> This particular marriage was "beautiful" (from supporting him through medical school, through breaking up a partnership to opening his solo ob-gyn practice), that is, beautiful until he decided also to dissolve this marriage because of the favors he has been receiving from the nurses nurturing this godlike feeling. (Tennessee)

> Many of the marital difficulties we have encountered have not been directly related to his practice but to his "dalliance" and impatience. (Pennsylvania)

I never minded his early calls, late calls, meetings—any of his many hours away from home—as long as I believed they were spent at the hospital at work. It was after I realized that he was fooling around that I resented it. We've never argued about this—or had words about it— but he knows I know—and although I really believe he's stopped, for me a trust has been broken, and it could never be the same. (Virginia)

I always said I would *not* marry a Dr. because their patients fall in love with them—they do. (New York)

I married him as a medical student. I was in graduate school after a master's degree. Marriage cut my career short. I did not mind. Had four children and was happy for over 10 years. Then he started playing around. He has not asked for a divorce, though I have considered it. He is a good father and provider but as a husband he is more like a brother and good friend. Hardly any love at all. Terrible temper. Always preoccupied with his work.

(Wyoming)

Having "remarried" my husband after he spent quite a few years indulging in extramarital affairs (usually of some duration & once more than one girlfriend at a time) I am ready to be courted and adored myself. (Florida)

My husband is currently a first-year resident in orthopedics, but unfortunately we are separated. Shortly after the birth of our second child he left me for a "younger" single. I am twenty-nine and she is twenty-five.

I have heard that many "new" doctors go through a phase such as this and was wondering if you have any information regarding this subject.

We were married while my husband was in med school. Incidentally, he attended the University of Bologna, so needless to say, we didn't have it too easy. But we were happy.

When we returned to the States we were still happy. Shortly before our son was born he started an affair with a girl from the hospital. Since then we have been back and forth, but now he has been out of the house for nine months. He has not made a move for divorce, and that is what leads me to believe it is the "young doctor's syndrome" I have heard so much about.

I hope I did not bore you with my story, but I thought you might have some information and know someone who can help me. (New York)

The one commonality in these sad letters is the resignation with which the wives accept their fates. They are willing to keep living with men who have abandoned them sexually and abused them emotionally. They have made the adjustment to humiliation and self-degradation that is required when sharing your life with a husband who pursues his own pleasures without regard for the effects on your psyche and self-esteem. Why do they stay? Security, family, hanging on to a status position they enjoy. All factors. But most of all, they can accept these conditions more easily than most women because doctors' wives have been conditioned to look upon infidelity as one of the special hazards of medical marriages. It is a pervasive fear they live with, an anticipated risk when one marries a physician. And since a good deal of living with a doctor involves compromise and acceding to his demands, how much more does it take to accept infidelity as just another of his ego-satisfying needs?

Every doctor's wife I spoke to admitted that doctors are exposed to greater temptations for extramarital relations than other groups of men. They hate the fact, they resist discussing it, and usually try to pretend it doesn't exist. The situation was clearly outlined by Dr. Robert E. Taubman in his article "Doctors and Marriages: Their Special Pressures," which appeared in *Medical World News*:

A problem peculiar to doctors is their many opportunities for adulterous affairs. Doctors are much sought after as husbands; they have status and high incomes. The result is that the average doctor will be the object of a lot of seductive female behavior. Furthermore, doctors are among the few professionals who can, by law and custom, disrobe their patients and examine their bodies in intimate detail. The entire doctor-patient relationship heightens the erotic fantasy about the doctor-healer. Don't kid yourself; it's tempting to go a step too far when examining an attractive nude woman, especially when the home life isn't so good. The doctor has to maintain careful defenses to preserve the integrity of the doctor-patient relationship.

When I brought up the subject of medical marital infidelity with one wife, she was furious. "Why does everyone think doctors play around more than other guys? Executives have secretaries who are crazy about them and chase them, too!" I then pointed out that whereas most offices are furnished with desks and file cabinets, hospitals are filled with beds, and whereas women in offices are fully clothed, patients in hospitals are not. The major distinction is that physicians inhabit an ambiance fraught with factors that are contributive to infidelity. And the wives know it. When this article, entitled "Doctors and Dalliance: Fact or Fiction?" appeared in *Medical/Mrs.* magazine, it evoked a spate of mail from women who concurred with the conclusions expressed.

> Physicians live in a special world with unusual circumstances that make them inclined to extramarital affairs or that make affairs a special temptation.
>
> A doctor's wife is locked out of many corners of that world. Both the hospital and the office are places apart where the physician is surrounded by women 90% of the time, whether they be patients, nurses or office personnel. The doctor's relationship with his women patients is, by its very nature, intimate, both physically and emotionally. And, though some may deny it, doctors' relationships with nurses are also often physically and emotionally intimate, though in different ways.

Medicine, as one doctor reminded me, is the only profession where men see women without their clothes every
day. Visual stimulation, usually needed for sexual awareness, is taken away for medical personnel because the
naked body is an everyday sight. Similarly, touch is more
common in the hospital than in everyday life. The very
nature of physical care requires touching the patient, and
the crowded quarters around a hospital bed, an office
examining room or a surgery table result in frequent physical contact between doctor and nurse.

If sight and touch are diminished as sources of arousal,
the verbal component to attraction remains, and it is here
that doctors and hospital personnel share a sense of intimacy. The nurse may know and see a side of a man
totally unknown to his wife, and sometimes she is around
him more than his wife is. Women in the hospital also
have a chance to judge the doctor as a man by how he be-
haves in a high pressure situation. And because they work
together in high pressure situations, doctors and nurses
often share an *esprit de corps* that the wife can neither
share nor understand.

It is probably this sense of sharing a small world that
accounts for the fact that the doctor who dallies rarely goes
in for a one-night stand. He is more inclined, say my interview sources, to become physically involved with someone
he knows, someone from the hospital or office. And because physical involvement builds on a closeness that already exists, emotional involvement usually follows. In
other words, the doctor is more likely to become involved
in a fairly long-term affair. And those jokes about doctors
and nurses may not be so funny—doctors do become involved with nurses.

If doctors have more temptation by the nature of their
work and the women who surround them, they also have
more opportunities for dalliance than most men. A banker
friend pointed out to me that he cannot, at 8:00 P.M.,
say to his wife, "The bank just called. I have to go. An
emergency." Nor do bankers or lawyers have beepers which

can be made to go off conveniently. One doctor spoke knowledgeably of Wednesday afternoon golf games that don't exist, nights out with the boys that cover for a romantic interlude. And doctors always have an excuse for being late—"I was at the hospital, tied up in the emergency room or the lab, or surgery." And for leaving early—"Hospital called. Sorry."

Aside from his daily routine, are there things about the physician, perhaps as a man himself, that make him more likely to play around? I asked the question several times and the answer almost uniformly was yes. Doctors seem to agree that they are more vulnerable to women on the make, partly because of ego needs. Men attracted to medicine as a career are necessarily egotistical; if not, they make ineffective physicians. But such egotistical men need more affirmation than others, and one doctor suggested they need adulation. Sex, he wrote, is certainly adulation!

If ego needs make some doctors vulnerable, their status as physicians makes them more appealing than some other men. Physicians have a certain reputation for prestige and success that makes them attractive to women. They also usually have enough money to treat a woman well. (Frequently, as one wife complained to me, they take a paramour to all the places the wife wanted to go for years!) Physicians are also considered "safe" by single women, in the sense that they will be fairly reliable, won't cause scenes and will be free of disease (one woman told me that doctors take lots of antibiotics!).

So there you have the physician—surrounded by women, with the freedom of time for an affair, in need of adulation and the target of propositions from lonely women. How do any of them ever resist? All the physicians I talked to agreed emphatically that whether or not a doctor will play around depends on the state of his marriage. When the marriage is going well, a doctor won't go out; if it's boring or strained, he's not happy at home and more likely to look around. A resident suggested that residency and internship are critical times in a marriage because the husband is never home. But when the husband's hours are long and irregular, the relationship may become strained, the wife may become demanding or a nag out of sheer frustration and loneliness. The husband, who works under pressure all day, is particularly sensitive to nagging, tension and discord at home. These problems may exist in any marriage, but medicine, with its pressures and temptations, exaggerates them.

Obviously, maintaining a happy medical marriage is a challenge and possibly a chore for the wife. Where most marital relationships are allowed to flounder and fluctuate and the wife can indulge in the luxury of being bitchy when the urge hits her, the medical wife has to maintain her guard to a degree. Because when the ordinary chap, like a lawyer, gets ticked off by a harassing wife, he goes to his office and works himself into sublimated oblivion, aided by a secretary who now refuses to even bring him coffee. But a doctor heads to his office or the hospital, where he is surrounded immediately by doting nurses and adoring patients who are just delighted with the opportunity to soothe his resentment or anger. There are unique conditions of intimacy that exist between doctors and nurses and doctors and female patients. Each of these relationships has a different emotional configuration; each is equally powerful in its sexual stimulation; each is equally conducive to infidelity.

The doctor/female patient symbiosis is one of "big daddy" and "trusting little girl" with a dash of sex thrown in to titillate the participants. No matter how old the woman, the doctor will greet her with, "How are you today, Sophie, honey? You're looking gorgeous," and will treat her with a pat-on-the-head familiarity that evokes a girlish giggle. After he leaves her bedside she gushes to her roommate: "Isn't he just wonderful?" Implicit in that statement is gratitude that the great man deigned to inquire about her well-being, and pride that *he* actually cares about little-

old-her. The physical examination wherein her body is
laid bare for his inspection and his hands probe her most
private areas creates a special feeling toward him, a sense
of almost wicked intimacy that he may or may not share.
But the choice is his.

A hospital patient's twenty-four-hour mission is watching and listening to her body, searching for signs of decay
or improvement, and thinking up a series of questions.
Her doctor is the man with the answers, and his bedside
appearance is the major highlight of the day. Every minute
he spends is pure gold, every word is heeded with rapt attention, and her appreciation of his attention is so intense
as to be almost pathetic. He is marvelous, talented, and
omniscient—the "best in his field" (ever notice how every
patient applies that epithet to his or her doctor?), and
there's nothing she would not do to earn his high opinion.

In the hospital, he moves about like a king, the center of
a retinue of genuflecting interns and reverential nurses who
report to him, answer his questions, and note down his
orders. He examines, listens, and commands. The emana-
tions of worship that surround him awe the patients and
project him into a powerful, unattainable figure. There are
few women patients who do not consciously or subconsciously try to seduce their doctors. And depending on how
attractive the woman, how determined her efforts, and how
receptive the physician, a liaison or at least a roll in the hay
is a strong possibility.

Then we have the male patient's wife. Her husband's life
is in the hands of the doctor; all her fears and hopes are
vested in his abilities, and her gratitude for his victories
in saving the man she loves invariably creates shock waves
of transference. As Dr. Brockman in *Brain Surgeon* put it,
"No wonder wives of patients fall in love with surgeons.
Aren't we the male who conquers her male?" She, too, sees
the adulatory aura that surrounds the doctor. She, too, lives

by the quality of his words and the tone of his voice. Though he may be insignificant-looking or downright ugly, to her he becomes a magnetic being of infinite power who at the moment controls her life. Add to that the fact that she is lonely, scared, going home to an empty house and bed, and you have a woman who is intensely vulnerable to any overtures the doctor chooses to make.

And now we come to the nurse/doctor affiliation: Nurses and doctors have a special relationship not unlike that of soldiers in a war. Fighting a side-by-side battle against death every day, they develop a close camaraderie that comes from shared anguish over failures and elation over successes. It is a powerful struggle that reduces all other facets of life to trivialities, and their mutual understanding creates a bond that cannot be equaled in any outside relationships. They develop an elitist sense of power that is the same primitive emotion that drives sex.

"There aren't many times I leave the operating room without at least a quarter of an erection," says Dr. Brockman. "Hell, why not? It's all totally primitive, isn't it? You're dealing with danger, blood, power, conquering the man or woman on the table. . . . I tell you, the man who isn't turned on by surgery is either a liar or a eunuch or both." Surgeons speak of the sexual drama of the operating room . . . the covered faces of the nurses leaving eloquent eyes exposed, the ballet effect of a large group of people skillfully choreographed to perform in perfect harmony. Given this highly sexually charged environment and the powerful adored guru figure of the physician, the inevitability of affairs between doctors and nurses is accepted as a given.

"I don't know why doctors get married at all," said Amanda R., a beautiful black nurse in the ICU of a major hospital. "All the doctors I know have their women right here. Maybe they need someone to run their houses, send out their laundry, and bring up their kids. But their real lives," she said emphatically, "are *here.*"

The *Medical Economics* survey offered a picture of the unfaithful doctor.

> Statistically, the most wandering eye belongs to a 50-year-old male surgical specialist who's been married 21 years to a wife who's now 47. They live in a Southern state with four teen-age children, two boys and two girls. The doctor is in fine shape physically, but emotionally, it's another story. He's pressed for time by a busy practice, doesn't enjoy life, and seldom gets home enough. When he is home, he and his wife disagree about how to spend their leisure hours together, and how the children should be raised, and about money. They try to discuss their differences rationally, but they have so little in common that it's as if they speak in different languages. They used to blow off steam by shouting, but now they give each other the silent treatment. Given such an unhappy home life, the doctor is vulnerable to an affair even if he's not actively seeking one.

Medical Economics also learned that most dallying doctors make their choices from hospital or office staffs. As doctors get older, they tend to "limit their affairs" to patients, office assistants, and family friends. Obviously they do not have to go very far to find willing partners. Not only does the doctor have this accessible group of females to indulge his carnal proclivities, but he is a prime target for predatory women who wish to indulge their upwardly mobile appetites. Since doctors are high on the "good catch" scale, with the appealing attendant affluence, they are courted by women and subjected to temptation constantly.

The physician offers a prestige position that many women covet. If he is undergoing any marital or family flack or just going through the midlife blahs, he is a prime target for seduction.

Gloria and Bob had been married for fifteen years. Bob came from a wealthy family, and Gloria's mother, a very forceful and controlling woman, had pushed her daughter into what she foresaw to be an advantageous union. Unfortunately, Bob had none of the drive and talent that had made his grandfather a millionaire, nor did he have any of the money that was controlled by his father. Gloria found herself beset with financial limitations that she detested and a diminishing regard for her husband, whom she viewed as a failure, especially compared to her best friend Charlotte's husband, Jim, who was a doctor. The two couples were very close and played bridge together once a week, went on vacations together, and spent a great deal of social time with each other. Then one winter night, Gloria took very ill, and they called Jim, of course. Who else would make a late-night house call but a friend? She had pneumonia and bedrest was prescribed. This was the first time Jim and Gloria spent time together, alone, unfettered by distracting spouses, and she made the most of it. Gloria had been briefed by Charlotte, in confidence, of course, on the daily marital problems in her household. Fully aware of how Jim's egotistical demands were met with continual resentment and resistance from his wife, Gloria was the soul of sympathetic compliance. Jim began dropping by during the day to check on his patient, and they had long "meaningful talks." After Gloria's recovery, which took far longer than necessary, the affair went into full swing. By the time Charlotte tuned in, it was too late and Gloria filed for divorce and Jim followed soon after. The moment they were married, Gloria plunged into the medical world with obvious delight. She joined the auxiliary and became a professional doctor's wife. Her mother was proudly approbative, her friends were admiringly envious. She positively basked in her new status and affluence and treated Jim with grateful adoration. It was a marvelously successful relationship. As Charlotte told her friends, Jim and Gloria had one major point in common: They both loved him.

The marital musical chairs that goes on in the medical world is recognized and feared by physicians' wives. Here is an article written by Anne Wang, who is the wife of a plastic surgeon, which appeared in *Medical/Mrs.* magazine:

Medical Meetings: I Fear What I'll Find

I am curious and fearful as I look for friends and associates after an interval of two years, not knowing what I will find in the way of survivors of the marital wars.

At least half seem to be divorced or in the process of marital breakup. Andy Moynihan, one of the best and the brightest, his choirboy's face unchanged under his greying hair, leans toward me.

"That's Bill's second wife? My God, she looks like a Madame!" I look in the direction he indicates. Raven hair frosted with white, and piled high with rhinestones, a black pantsuit cut too low at the neckline and too tight in the crotch and the buttocks, she is as conspicuous in this roomful of conservatively dressed wives as a Moslem at a Jewish wedding. The room, too large for this small group, is harshly lit, and full of sharp planes and angles. It does not spare her. Like Andy, I find myself missing the quiet presence of Jean.

Why all this marital restlessness? Are doctors, like actors and TV executives, a high-risk group? Do long-married medical couples compose a survivor's society, like Donner Pass trekkers, or Sherpa guides for Annapurna?

Paradoxically, the breakups don't seem to come during the high pressure days of medical school and residency, when emergency calls and board examinations loom over us all like the Himalayas, but rather later, when our long-delayed hopes for the good life materialize into reality. Do too many wives strive each day to build intimacy with a partner who has already spent his diurnal currency of emotion? Or is his self-protective anesthesia one he tries to turn off and can't?

But not all physician adultery leads to divorce. Dissolution of their marriages is not the preferred route, and doctors actually have a lower divorce rate than that of the general population. As reported in *California Medicine*, an "analysis of 57,514 initial complaints for divorce, separate maintenance and annulment filed in California during the first six months of 1968 reveals that physicians are considerably less prone to marital failure than men of comparable age in the general population." And as an interesting sidelight, "orthopedists and psychiatrists have possibly the highest rate of marital demise."

Doctors tend to be conservative, and abandoning the sacrament of marriage is not a step they take lightly. But perhaps an even larger deterrent to breaking connubial ties is the financial penalty involved. Doctors have the largest disposable income of any professional group in the country; they also have the least amount of business experience. This wealth-without-know-how is a devastating combination in the world of finance, and Wall Street abounds in stories about doctors' investment debacles. As a result of constant legal tax evasion machinations, their finances are often massively convoluted and entwined with their wives. And today, with the high risk of malpractice suits, doctors are going more and more in the direction of placing major portions of their assets in their wives' names. A divorce would wreak havoc with these complicated arrangements and conceivably leave the physician penniless. There are possibly more medical marriages held together today by financial ties than by emotional ones.

The doctor's wife, too, has many reasons for resisting divorce. Simply, she likes the good life, the club, home, the easy flow of money, and the social status. If her life is heavily involved with her husband's profession, she's active in volunteer groups and many other medically affiliated organizations. If she were to dissolve her marriage, she would be losing not only a husband but a good portion of her social life and identity. Here is a letter from a doctor's wife who bemoans the loss of her position which occurred due to death rather than divorce, but the resultant effect was identical:

> I am a recently widowed doctor's wife. My problem? Where do *we* fit in? Having been part of medical life and world, loving it—it is suddenly over.

When that letter appeared in *Medical/Mrs.*, the response was tremendous.

> I would like to urge her to join the County Medical Society Auxiliary in her area. There she will continue to be a member of the medical world, will find widows with whom she can share and contribute and most of all she will give her life some purpose again. Any doctor's wife can tell her how and where to join and she will find her membership most welcome.

And here's a letter that gives you an idea of the lasting identity doctors' wives feel with their husbands' profession.

> Let us start a Medical Widows Club. I would love to hear from all you doctors' widows. I promise to answer all letters as I am lonesome for the old life too.

Both the doctors and their wives often have a strong, selfish interest in preserving their marriages, no matter what the condition. Moreover, doctors have a fantastic built-in mechanism for denial that enables them to accept what others would consider untenable situations. Secure in their exalted status, they convince themselves easily that any difficulties in their marriages are merely minor peccadilloes that follow the national norm. And affairs? Why, these little adventures actually help their marriages by removing some of the responsibility for sexual satisfaction from their wives.

"I'm healthy and happy now," says a Texas urologist to *Medical Economics*. He reports that poor sexual relations with his wife used to give him a pervasive feeling of discontent. "I had an affair with a nurse and it was wonderful. Today I think better of my marriage and I'm having a ball!"

The smug self-involvement in that statement is typical of a doctor who sees women as servants of his needs. It exhibits a myopic egotism that comes from years of dealing with people on unreal terms wherein awareness of their sensibilities never clouds his picture. The absence of any allusion to his wife's feelings about their poor sexual relations and implicit disavowal of his role in that failure, the self-satisfied reference to the wonderfulness of his affair with the nurse, omitting any reference to her feelings in being used to shore up his faltering masculinity, the unilateral conclusion that "I think better of my marriage," as though his opinion alone is all that matters in this usually dual relationship, and finally the repellently adolescent macho statement "I'm having a ball" all add up to the picture of an egotistical emotional cripple who could never have a genuine relationship with any woman.

The doctor's supreme egoism also produces a marvelous inner drive for self-justification of his extramarital activities. "Indeed some doctors do find that affairs can supply an essential spice to an otherwise substantial but bland life of marriage." Nearly 58 percent of the unfaithful doctors believe they have successfully concealed their amours from their spouses. Yet, given his extreme insensitivity, how could a doctor recognize whether his wife has learned of his infidelity? For unless she actually confronts him with her knowledge or suspicions, he is woefully ill-equipped to read the subtle signs that indicate the hurt and humiliation she suffers. A great many doctors' wives choose to avoid any open discussion of their husbands' extramarital activities because it suits their needs to maintain a façade of ignorance. For she, too, develops a personal marital survival mechanism that blocks out awareness of his infidelities by subconsciously relegating all indications to below the level of her cognizance. At the same time, she amplifies all the assets of his conjugal attributes—good provider, good doctor, respected community position, fine social companion—and a satisfactory state of marriage is thereby achieved. She builds a life based on compromises of her own choice, and as long as the arrangement is acceptable to both partners, it works. But sometimes third-party interference can destroy the carefully constructed harmony.

Bea and Eric came to the United States from Holland soon after Eric completed his medical schooling at the University of Leiden. He had been offered a residency in vascular surgery at a major Detroit hospital and was excited at this superb opportunity to learn from one of the greatest surgeons in the specialty and to live in Detroit. Bea shared his pride in the achievement of being selected for this sought-for opportunity but not his enthusiasm for moving to the United States. She was a simple, gentle young woman who loved the small Dutch town in which she had been born and envisioned spending the rest of her life there, happily growing old among friends and family as the wife of a respected physician. However, she reckoned without Eric's powerful drive and ambition. Unlike Bea, he came from a poor family and was the first member to go on to higher education. Bea's upper-middle-class parents were rather uncomfortable with this intense young man, whom they regarded as somewhat crude and socially unsuitable for their gently reared daughter. Eric had campaigned to capture Bea with the same aggressive assumption of success with which he approached all his goals, and, of course, he won as always.

Bea and Eric moved into a tiny apartment in Detroit and Eric disappeared into the hospital for eighteen-hour work days, leaving Bea to find her way around the frightening city. Her initial adaptation was difficult, as Bea was terrified and painfully lonely. In time, she became immersed in the hospital auxiliary and the kind of good work she had been trained to do in Holland. Then children came, and they moved to a suburban house where Bea could garden and be a contented homemaker and mother, a role that suited her perfectly. Eric's drive and talent soon took him to a position of prominence in his profession and he became a full professor, head of the department, and a sought-after speaker by medical groups throughout the world. Bea did not mind his absences because she had developed a major new interest—the church. A few years before, their youngest daughter took seriously ill with a rare infection from a bacteria that the doctors were unable to isolate. Forced to abandon her belief in the medical profession, Bea turned to prayer and made a vow to God that if her daughter survived, she would devote the rest of her life to the service of the church. The child recovered and Bea became a devout woman.

Eric was a vital, attractive man who had a series of liaisons with nurses and patients throughout his married life. In fact, he was never without one. He loved Bea, but this quiet, plain-looking religious woman was no foil for his exuberant social and sexual appetites. He found his home a comfortable place that provided a stabilizing fulcrum for his frenetic existence. He did not want to hurt Bea or to disturb the satisfying status quo, and fully believed he concealed his extramarital activities from her. What he did not know was that his success in maintaining the secret of his promiscuity was as much due to Bea's self-induced purblindness as to his direction. She had built a life based on strong beliefs—in her husband and the church—and she could not accept any weakness in either. Both Eric and Bea were quite contented with the three faces of their life, which consisted of his life, her life, and their life together. He was free to go his way unhindered by wifely demands; she was consumed by her commitment to the church and was pleased to have minimal connubial demands interfere with her activities; and both enjoyed sharing a fine home and having a suitable companion for social occasions.

And then Eric turned fifty. Suddenly he began to notice that the doctors who called him "Sir" were not all that young anymore. And the deference from hospital personnel that he used to accept as the due of his lofty position, he began attributing to his advancing age. When he took Bea to a medical association dinner, he was conscious of her sedate graying appearance and felt a displeasure at the middle-aged look she conferred on them as a couple. When he came into the office the next morning, there was a new young receptionist behind the desk who looked at him with awe and admiration and he liked the feeling of being the sexually attractive man he saw reflected in her eyes. She was twenty-seven and very pretty. First they had lunch together in the hospital cafeteria. Then he started stopping at her house for a drink, and soon the relationship had grown into a full-blown love affair. But this one was unlike all those amours that had come before, because now for the first time Eric was the insecure partner. She was so young and lovely and he was this middle-aged man with the inevitable signs of aging. It went on for a few months and Bea's internal denial device went into full swing so that all signs of Eric's infidelity were rendered invisible to her.

It might have petered out by normal attrition, but the young woman was determined to capture the title of Mrs. Doctor. When she told Eric that she was pregnant, his first reaction was pride. He was so delighted to have this tangible proof of his virility that the consequences did not even enter his mind. When his young lover talked about marriage, he was stunned at first. After all, he had a wife. As the picture began to shape up in his mind, a stunning young wife with a young child by his side, he liked the cloak of youthfulness invested in him by this new family grouping. He hated to hurt Bea, for whom he had a genuine affection, but the pull of his own ego plus the unrelenting pressure from the mother-to-be was too much. Bea filed for divorce and Eric remarried one month before the child was born.

Bea was not emotionally damaged by Eric's defection any more than she was by his many adulterous deceptions, since she looked upon his behavior as manifestations of weakness and loss of faith. Not all women are fortunate enough to possess a strong religious belief that enables them to cope with personal torment. The recourse for many doctors' wives who feel abandoned by husbands who are uninterested, inattentive and/or unfaithful is extramarital relationships.

The *Medical Economics* 1973 life-style survey turned up the fact that one out of twelve physicians' wives questioned admitted to infidelity. In itself, this is a striking statistic. Even more significant is the doctor's response to the question of how he would react to the knowledge that his wife was straying from the marital bed. The responses were varied as to the exact procedures each doctor would choose to initiate but similar in general reaction as to how it would affect his psyche. The consensus: He wouldn't really care.

Here are some specific responses *Medical Economics* received from doctors on the matter of dealing with their wives' infidelity:

> As a couple, we're incompatible. We have no similar likes or dislikes. So if my wife fooled around, I just wouldn't care—I'd look the other way.

As the years go by, my wife raises more and more grievances against me and never lets the sun go down on her anger. I'd be happy if she had an affair—but I wouldn't let on I knew.

I'd shoot to kill if I learned that my wife was screwing around.

It wouldn't bother me, I'd join in as a voyeur.

In Latin or Islamic society, flogging, stoning, or death is the punishment meted out to adulterous women. A husband's honor is measured by the behavior of his wife, and there is no more reviled, scorned male than the cuckold who is disdained as a weakling who cannot control even his own family. In our society, a man whose wife has been unfaithful feels the pain of inadequacy, a sense of failure in his performance as a mate and lover, and the deep anger of betrayal. A doctor is spared all these agonies of guilt and self-doubt.

That unflappable ego and immutably secure belief in his own value enables him to attribute his wife's infidelity to her aberration alone. He does not regard her actions as reactive to him but merely due to her private neuroses. How could her misbehavior be motivated by his weakness as a lover or his failure as a companion? Everyone adores him, everyone respects his knowledge and admires his strength and power. Ergo: If his wife must resort to outside stimuli to bring her happiness when she is blessed with the most prized and enviable connubial conditions, then she is obviously sick.

A wife who longs for affection and caring and then finds herself unable to communicate these feelings and expectations to a husband who cannot comprehend her needs or even consider the possibility of his own limitations is filled with frustration and anger. There is no more devastating response to a plea for love than indifference, and doctors' wives who cannot reach or touch their husbands will often be driven to desperate measures to gain attention. Overt adultery is a frequent weapon.

Nora was an extremely vivacious woman and the youngest of three daughters. When she met Dick, he had just joined a successful group practice as an orthopedist and was considered the most eligible catch in town. He was a sweet, soft-spoken man who internalized all his emotions and was dedicated to his profession.

Shy and reserved in manner himself, he was instantly captivated by Nora's high-powered animation and they were married shortly thereafter and settled into a standard suburban existence that Nora enjoyed enormously. Her personality was characterized by a volatility that verged on the manic and she needed attention and affection constantly. She developed friendships of such major intensity that they usually burned out because of the excesses of her giving and the reciprocal demands she then imposed. To Nora's utter joy, she had a baby within two years, and then two more in successive years. Motherhood was ideal for Nora. She was busy and had soft, cuddly, helpless beings who depended on her and on whom she could lavish all the intensity of her affection. Dick worked long hours and became involved in teaching in the local medical school hospital. He loved his wife and family, and as long as Nora was wrapped up in her babies, she was content with the limited time and attention Dick gave them. Life went along satisfactorily until the children all reached school age. Suddenly she was not needed anymore and she missed the malleable babies she could control. No longer a full-time mother, she reverted to being a wife and looked to Dick to fill the voids created by the children's new independence. She started complaining when he came home late, then nagging when he phoned that he had emergencies, then making scenes when he left home in the evenings to make rounds. Dick was surprised by her outbursts and then annoyed. Of course his work came first; the fact that patients take priority, Dick felt, is basic in a medical marriage, and he looked upon Nora's resentments as immature and unrealistic. Unable to communicate to Dick her feelings of despair and rejection, she turned to outside sources. Nora had her first affair with a neighbor with whom she worked on a community council. As she did with every project, Nora threw herself into the affair with excessive abandon. She was "in love," replete with fluttering heart when he came through the door, and listened eagerly to his every word with complete rapture. She wanted to know all about him, how he thought and felt on every issue in life. He was, of course, flattered to death. It was a long time since anyone, if ever, had shown that much interest in him, and he loved it.

But soon, her intensity became wearing, and then alarming as he realized she was acting with little discretion. She apparently did not care if her husband knew of the affair; in fact, she seemed to want him to know. If Dick was aware of Nora's infidelity, he did not show it. Yet it would have been impossible to live in the same house without knowing of her feelings. Her whispered phone calls, the infatuated way she hung on her lover's arm when he came to pick her up to attend the community meetings, were signs that even a minimally observant person could not miss. Dick continued to be polite, busy, and dutiful, and apparently totally unconcerned with his wife's extracurricular activities. The affair broke up when the man's wife threatened him with divorce, and with an outward display of great sorrow and an inner feeling of great relief, he told Nora he could not hurt his family and the relationship had to end.

Nora went on to another affair and then another, and never did Dick acknowledge the existence of any lovers, or flaws in his perfect marriage. No matter how extreme her behavior or how blatant her infidelities, he continued to perform his professional and marital duties in the same sweet, detached, and efficient manner. His reputation in the community was excellent, he was respected by his peers, and greatly beloved by his patients and nurses. He had a lovely home, an attractive wife, and three nice children. As far as he was concerned, life was idyllic and he chose to ignore any evidence to the contrary.

The deprivation of response and emotion from her husband was driving Nora to hyperintensities that verged on self-destruction. Then one night they attended a local party and the host had invited two young priests who were on their way to a vacation and were dressed in sports clothes as were the other guests. Nora immediately attached herself to the more attractive of the two and began to drink heavily with him and make strong sexual overtures. Soon everyone at the party became aware of the drama, and the tone of the evening became strained as they realized Nora's purpose.

It was inconceivable that Dick did not see her behavior, and yet he was the only one there who seemed relaxed and unconcerned. Nora went back to the bar to get still another drink and announced loudly, "Want to bet that I can get the Father to fuck me before the evening's over?" An hour later, she and the priest disappeared into the adjoining garage, and with everyone miserably, uncomfortably aware of the situation, she consummated her bet on the back seat of the host's BMW.

It was a night that affected everyone who had been at the party and one that none would forget. Especially Nora, who now had to face the fact that her screams would never be heard by Dick. She knew that his denial mechanism enabled him to see their marriage and family with a selective vision that blocked out any doubts about his performance as a husband and father. Now she realized that he was emotionally incompetent or unwilling to comprehend her need for love and affection and that any effort she made to get his attention, no matter how drastic, would be discounted or ignored. The next lover was a serious one who left his wife in order to marry Nora. When she sued for divorce, no one was surprised except Dick.

The unfair aspect of the whole sordid mess was that Dick emerged with a pure, untarnished image and Nora was castigated by the community. The picture presented was one of the fine, kindly doctor being victimized by a neurotic, bitchy, dissatisfied wife, and his contributions to the destruction of the marriage remained invisible. The fact that he constantly ignored her bizarre behavior was attributed to his noble tolerance and understanding instead of being recognized as the response of a distant, uncaring husband who continued to ignore his wife's pleas for help.

In a paper on "The Doctor's Wife: Mental Illness and Marital Pattern," published in the International Journal of Psychiatry in Medicine, 1975, the doctor-husbands of the women who were undergoing psychiatric treatment were reported to be

successful in demeaning the legitimate and meaningful feelings expressed by their wives by labeling them "emotional outbursts" and making demands for more "logical and rational" methods of problem-solving. Their need to avoid open conflict appears paramount and may, in part, explain such phenomena as:

1. Prescribing medication for the wife. Physicians, when queried about this practice, are usually defensive and offer as excuses such statements as "I'd do anything to keep her happy and get her off my back!"

2. Increasing the amount of time spent in practice which effectively removes him from the arena of conflict.

3. Tolerating the increasingly outrageous behavior the angry wife often resorts to as her needs continue to be unmet.

The poverty of communication between the marital partners is striking and they often impress the interviewer as virtual strangers, sharing only accommodations and children.

Of the seventy-six wives who gave information as to whether their husbands met their emotional needs, ninety-two percent indicated that these needs were not met.

The double standard that judges the adulterous wife corrupt and the adulterous husband misunderstood is intensified in medical marriages. Here is this marvelous man, this godlike figure out there saving lives and ministering to the sick, and providing his wife with the considerable fruits of his labors so that she can sit around the pool making illicit assignations in between trips to the department stores and the beauty salon. The emotional deprivation that the doctor imposes on his wife and the self-withdrawal with which he responds to her pleas for intimacy are hidden causal factors that the public never sees. The doctor's wife is not a sympathetic figure. Perceived by the community as the possessor of all the elements of the perfect life without having made any contributions to merit it, her adulterous transgressions are regarded with contempt and her fall from grace with ill-veiled envious glee. And the good doctor sails through untouched, forever beloved, respected, and admired.

VII

Escape from What?
Alcoholism and Addiction

"Why did he do it? He had *everything* to live for," said friends and neighbors sadly as they returned from the funeral of Dr. Kenneth Martin. The cause of death was a combination of Demerol and bourbon, both taken in such massive doses as to plainly indicate intent, especially when the victim is a physician who is aware of the lethal effects of such a mixture. Why, indeed, would a succesful pediatrician who is loved by his young patients, adored by their mothers, and liked by his colleagues have taken his own life?

His bereaved wife seemed stunned and numb. "It's the shock," said people sympathetically. Of course, Dr. Martin's medical associates recognized Dee's glazed look and incoherent behavior as manifestations of her acute alcoholism. And the two Martin children, Tom, aged seventeen, and Alicia, aged sixteen, looked straight ahead in bleak silence as everyone tried to console them for having lost a wonderful father. The children heard little because they were both totally stoned on Darvon.

The abysmal wreckage of the Martin family offers a classic case of the pressures and psychosocial factors that drive a doctor to self-destruction and his family to despair.

Ken Martin entered medical school with great pride in his achievement and anticipation of a golden future. The child of working-class parents, he was the first member of his family to ever go on to higher education. He had a powerful longing for upward mobility and a strong desire to make a visibly important contribution to mankind, the world, or in some way improve the human condition. Ken loved children and they responded to him, so it was natural for him to go into pediatrics. The first day he walked into the hospital as an intern was the most memorable day of his life; it was as though everything he had ever done was building toward this moment. When the hospital elevator doors opened, the man next to him, noting the stethoscope Ken had spent ten minutes placing with studied casualness in his pocket, moved aside and said deferentially, "You first, doctor." Ken felt he would never in his life be happier than at that minute. During the next few years, he grew to love the excitement of the hospital, the romance of medicine, the status his position brought him. Dealing with emergency cases of critically ill children and dangerously afflicted infants was enormously challenging, albeit exhausting. Life was full and thrilling. Then he met and fell in love with Dee, who was a pediatrics nurse in the hospital, and they were married when he completed his residency. Ken was now ready to reap the rewards of his years of training and dedication; he applied for and was accepted as an associate in an excellent, lucrative medical group practice in an affluent Ohio suburb. Ken and Dee bought a lovely house and settled into the community with all the expectation of enjoying the good life. And for many years, they did. The children arrived in proper order, first Tom and then Alicia. Ken was esteemed by everyone; Dee was busy with the Garden Club, PTA, and community affairs.

Ken could not pinpoint the exact moment he began to feel dissatisfaction and a sense of personal failure. It started as boredom as his practice took on a day-by-day sameness.

No excitement of critically ill patients being brought in for diagnosis, cure, and often lifesaving surgery, as he had experienced at the hospital. None of the exhilaration of success when a dying child survived due to his ministrations. Or the depths of anguish when he had to tell parents their child cannot live. In his private practice, all Ken saw was well-cared-for, basically upper-class children with an occasional case of flu, chicken pox, or diarrhea. His work became tedious and unfulfilling and he began to experience bouts of dispirited emptiness. So he drove himself to work harder and longer. When a hysterical mother called at 2:00 A.M. to report her baby had spiked a fever, he didn't tell her to give the child aspirin and phone him again in the morning—he got dressed and drove over, although it usually turned out to be a minor matter that disappeared within hours. When he had trouble with fatigue the day after a night call, he hit on the idea of taking a shot of Demerol and found that gave him the lift he needed to get through the day. When he got home at night, usually late because his working hours seemed to get longer and longer as he felt compelled to visit his hospitalized patients two and three times a day and see every child whose mother reported a symptom, Ken would fall into his favorite chair with a tall glass of bourbon "to unwind," as he told Dee. She would usually join him and it became commonplace for their children to come down for breakfast in the morning and find their parents asleep in the living room next to empty liquor bottles. Ken found a shot of Demerol helped relieve the headache and nausea of his hangover so that he could function the next day.

Dee began to drop out of many of her community activities. A rather weak and dependent person, she had always relied on Ken's strength and sense of purpose to direct their lives. Now she felt disoriented and lost as Ken seemed to drift away from her. His erratic ups and downs frightened her; he was positive and jovial one second and irritable and unapproachable the next. And their sex life had become nonexistent as Ken became entirely impotent. She had started to drink with Ken, and finding that liquor helped her get through the day, began drinking in the early evening, then the afternoon and then the morning.

Then Alicia had some serious difficulties in school and her teacher called to suggest that the child could use some help. Dee became upset and said she would discuss it with her husband. But when she talked to Ken about the problem, he dismissed the matter as a minor difficulty that Alicia would overcome in time. And then Tom was brought home one night by the police who had found him selling amphetamines in the school parking lot, but seeing he was Dr. Martin's son, they let him off with a warning. Ken and Dee were shaken when they realized Tom had been systematically stealing drugs from his father and selling them. Two weeks later, Alicia totaled her car when driving under the influence of drugs.

By now, Ken's problems with alcohol had become apparent to his associates, although they were unaware of his addiction to Demerol. Everyone liked Ken tremendously; he was charming and affable, even more so when he was buoyed by alcohol and Demerol. The nursing staff at the hospital began to report episodes of Ken's inappropriate bizarre behavior, and finally his colleagues became concerned with the danger he posed to patients and to the reputation of their group practice and they called him in for a confrontation. Ken denied emphatically that he was an alcoholic, because he truly believed he wasn't. No one had ever accused him of that because who would think of making such a charge against a respected physician? "Look, I just take a few drinks when I'm beat. Doesn't everyone?" He was told he would be on probation, and if another incident was reported, he would regretfully be fired from the group. He swore he could lick it. He didn't *need* a drink—it was just a social thing.

When he got home that night at 10:00, he found Dee in a stupefied sleep in front of the TV set. Neither of the children was home, although it was a week night and they had been told school nights required a nine-o'clock curfew. When they arrived home at 1:00 A.M., they found their mother still asleep in the living room and their father on the couch, dead.

The tragedy of the Martins is not a rare occurrence in medical families, yet it inevitably evokes incredulity from friends and neighbors. "They seemed such a nice, normal family. The doctor was such a lovely man." The disaster is even more perplexing to people whose daily lives are spent battling the normal anxieties that beset advertising executives who risk losing their jobs when the agency loses an account, stock brokers whose income are controlled by the vagaries of the Dow-Jones and the economy, and all other business people who suffer the fears and insecurities of fluctuating fiscal conditions that never trouble physicians. As seen by the ordinary mortal, doctors live a charmed, enviable existence, immune from the tribulations that trouble the rest of us.

A medical school administrator, addressing the incoming class, asked them, "Do you know what people will call the student who ends up at the bottom of the class? Doctor!" The point is, once he gets that magic title, his status is assured as well as his income. A doctor today is assured of a secure financial future and the respect of the community. Every morning he embarks on his work day with the ego-gratifying certainty that he will pass his time in a dominant position over everyone he encounters and will be treated only with respect if not adoration. No boss will chew him out because sales are dropping, no client will call him up to harangue him about unsatisfactory service, no customer will cancel a major order because delivery was late. None of the demeaning and dispiriting assaults on the psyche that most people endure almost daily will ever happen to a physician.

And the power of his pedestal position will carry over to his wife, who will be welcomed with honor everywhere. Those commonplace concerns over bills and worries about the mounting cost of living will never cause domestic quarrels or sleepless nights. In short, in the eyes of the rest of the world, the doctor has it made. What could drive a man who lives such a seemingly trouble-free existence into the neurotic need for alcohol or drugs? The usual user is a desperate seeker of escape from the rigors of his reality. What in that roseate life picture is the doctor escaping from?

To understand that, we must first consider the doctor's personality, motivations, and goals. The reasons for entering the medical profession could be the desire for status and wealth, the need to dominate and exercise power, the wish to help people and make contributions to the welfare and well-being of mankind. The degree to which these motivations and goals are satisfied will determine the doctor's state of mind and happiness, as it does with most people. But doctors are not most people. The compulsive obsessive aspects of their personalities make their reactions more excessive. And the intensity of their training makes the disappointment over failure of expectations so much more acute. An engineer was discussing their comparative schooling experience with a doctor friend: "Where was your training any different from mine? We're both just technicians, except that I deal with machines and you with people." The doctor said emphatically, "There's no way you can compare your or anybody's schooling to medicine. Two cataclysmic emotional things happened to me in school that could never have occurred in your school. One, I was instrumental in causing a man to die. Two, I saved a woman's life."

The young doctor who starts out in private practice already has been subjected to soul-searching experiences that alternately drained and elated him; he has dealt with the most basic elements of life—fear, survival, and death. It is natural that when he emerges from training, the extent of his expectations is in direct proportion to the emotional expanse of his experiences. But he may be doomed to disappointment. Of the almost 450,000 doctors in the United States, how many are truly leaving an imprint on the world? A great deal of private practice today is mundane and unchallenging, largely involving prescribing for the control of chronic ailments. Other than surgery, there are few opportunities for achieving the nobility of purpose that the young medical student envisions in his future. The romantic image of being a doctor is one that excites him as he first enters the hospital in the symbolic white coat. But romanticism disappears with familiarity, and excitement palls with time; being called "doctor" becomes an ordinary salutation rather than a thrilling accolade.

The average doctor is reduced to the role of technician, but he is ever conscious of the fact that it is a human body—and human life—he is working with and minor errors can cause major catastrophes. This puts him under special strain at all times. He works very long hours because his income is dependent on piece work. Unlike manufacturers, lawyers, and executives who derive income from the labors of others as well as their own, a doctor's earnings are determined by the number of people he treats. When he isn't occupied with seeing patients, he must read the huge number of medical journals that pile up on his desk daily in order to keep up with new developments and drugs. He becomes a man absorbed by his profession, yet not necessarily fulfilled by it. His total preoccupation with medicine leaves him no time for broadening cultural and social interests and he becomes a very boring, dull, and limited person, which makes him a growing disappointment to his wife and frequently a failure to his family.

According to Drs. Herbert C. Modlin and Alberto Montes of the famed Menninger Foundation, the reasons for physicians' becoming drug addicts are "(1) discouragement regarding the anticipated rewards of medical practice; (2) disillusionment in their expectations to gain succor and satisfaction in their marriage; and (3) inability to grow into the traditional role of father and achieve satisfaction as a parent from the parent-child relationship." A study of narcotics addiction in doctors done at the Menninger Clinic turned up that most addiction appears after about ten years of practice when the dull reality of their lives becomes apparent. Sustained in their earlier years by great expectations, they move from "adolescent fantasy to courtship, to marriage to parenthood." Once they reach the terminus of their dreams, then "disillusionment and reactive regression sets in."

All kinds of people suffer disappointments and disillusionments. Why then do so many doctors resort to drugs and alcohol to cope with these strains? The numbers are overwhelming. The rate of drug addiction among doctors is estimated to be thirty times that of the general population. And doctors make up 15 percent of the drug addicts in the country. At the Menninger Clinic, about half of the addicts admitted for treatment are doctors. The answer is simple—accessibility and familiarity. Drugs are so available to doctors and their dispensing so much part of their lives that the temptation to use drugs for temporary fast relief of even minor problems becomes seductive.

It starts at medical school when late hours and around-the-clock duty forces a student to take drugs to keep awake. And it often develops into a pleasant and then necessary crutch that he continues in private practice. Perhaps he has a few straight nights of being on call and feels absolutely beat the next days, there are all those handy amphetamines around, so he pops a pill or two. Twenty-three percent of medical students have used amphetamines more than once, and 15 percent continue to use them after their clinical years begin. If the doctor is really "down," Demerol is right there to pick up his mood and get him through treatment and rounds, so he takes a shot "just this once" and feels great; Demerol takes effect almost instantly and produces a marvelous flying feeling of euphoria. An estimated 90 percent of all doctor-addicts are on Demerol; the other popular physician popper-uppers are Talwin and Darvon.

It's all so easy and available. And it fits into the current medical method of handling emotional and physical discomfort—prescribing medication for instant relief. Migraine? Take Cafergot. Tension? Take Valium. Constipation? Take Colase. Patients come to doctors with the firm expectation that they will leave with prescriptions for drugs that will take care of their ailments. For the doctor, chemical solutions to all problems seem the way to go, and giving himself a quick shot when he's depressed or weary seems natural. The relief is so immediate as to justify his act because isn't that what a good doctor does, relieves pain as quickly as possible? "I don't really need it," he deludes himself, "but it will certainly help me through this one." And then he finds himself repeating the procedure whenever exhaustion or anxiety appears, until insidiously and unintentionally he slips into addiction.

Addiction—the very word is an anathema to a doctor, and accepting that epithet for himself is impossible. His ego-bound image of himself places him high up there among the important and admired people, not down in the Harlem tenements and Bowery streets where one finds addicts and alcoholics. And so he denies. "Physicians rely on rationalization and denial constantly," says the *New England Journal of Medicine.*

This absolute denial of dependency on drugs and alcohol

is even a larger problem than the addiction itself. The pedestal position of physicians has been so deeply ingrained in the individuals as well as the hierarchy of the medical profession that it is extremely difficult for them to admit to any such tawdry human frailties as alcoholism and drug addiction. The very words make them wince when used in conjunction with their esteemed colleagues, so they have invented a respectable euphemism to be used for those ill comrades who they believe have temporarily succumbed to weakness: They are called "impaired physicians." Not for the physician the seedy term *drunk* or *junky*, he is merely *impaired*. Lulled by the mild medical terminology for his damaged condition and by his own narcissism, the impaired doctor disdains criticism or help since he regards his addiction as dangerous in minor mortals but certainly within the control of so masterful a person as himself. "I can stop anytime I wish," he will aver. He believes it so strongly that it is easy for him to convince family, friends, and associates.

A Wisconsin gynecologist began treating his headaches with Percodan. Within two years he was taking four hundred pills a day, a habit that forced him to fly from state to state in search of new supplies of the drug. Finally, he was arrested, and "as they handcuffed me," he said, "I thought, Why are they doing this? I don't really have a problem."

A prominent California dermatologist arranged to meet a colleague for coffee. At 9:00 A.M. the next morning, they had coffee and during the course of the interview he had to get up twice to go out and inject himself with Talwin. He was addicted and was injecting himself every thirty minutes. Yet he did not consider himself an addict. Unfortunately, a physician's habit gets bigger and bigger because he has such an unlimited supply of drugs that in order to keep going he has to inject higher and higher doses in order to maintain the effect. The street-level addict is injecting 3 to 7 percent heroin, and the physician addict is injecting 100 percent morphine, 100 percent Demerol, 100 percent Talwin.

Medical Economics found that doctors' powerful built-in denial mechanism was highly operative in the responses they received to their survey on physicians' life-styles.

One of the basic tenets of Alcoholics Anonymous is that you can't begin to solve your problem until you admit you have one. Perhaps this reluctance to face up to the problem of alcohol or drug abuse is why the files of so many local medical societies are filled with stories of failure regarding attempts to help impaired physicians.

Despite AMA estimates that close to 10 percent of all doctors will have a drinking problem at some time in their lives, only three out of 100 doctors in our survey admit to overusing alcohol. The figures on drug use are even more dramatic: Only two in 1,000 physicians say they overuse hard drugs, while AMA studies show that 1 to 2 percent of all physicians are drug abusers, adding that "drug addiction among physicians appears to be an occupational hazard."

Surveyed doctors who do admit to overuse problems, however, often unfold tales of broken marriages, failing health, and various legal entanglements. The hopelessness and despair common to most of these doctors is capsuled by a Mississippi GP who says "My family life has been a nightmare for the past 10 years because of my drinking and because I was often under the influence of mood-changing drugs. I'm now under a doctor's care, but staying sober is still proving to be a serious problem."

A Louisiana psychiatrist describes the effect that too much drinking has had on his life in these terms: "Booze has completely disrupted my family life. The estrangement from my children is something I'll always regret."

Dependence on alcohol and drugs can have even worse side effects. Alcoholism, for example, is considered a major factor in the 100 or more physician suicides committed every year. The child of an alcoholic parent is five to 10 times more likely to become an alcoholic than other children. Of course, the most serious implication is that the impaired physician who continues to practice could ultimately be responsible for the injury or death of a patient.

While no meaningful correlation regarding drug abuse can be drawn from our survey because of the small number of doctors indicating a problem in that area, it's possible to develop a profile of the alcohol-impaired doctor. He's likely to be older, has what he terms to be a "lousy" marriage, feels he isn't getting enough enjoyment out of life, and doesn't consider himself to be in the best of health. Among specialties, GPs, FPs, and psychiatrists are most likely to overuse alcohol. There are more overusers—and drinkers in general—in the Northeast.

Doctors in the West are most likely to have a son or daughter with an alcohol problem. But a number of doctors admit that they have no idea whether their children use, much less overuse, alcohol or drugs. One reason for this information gap could be the amount of time most doctors spend away from home. More than one-fourth of our respondents complain they're "not home enough," and when asked what mistake they'd made in raising their children, their most frequent response is "not spending enough time with them."

The methods used by physicians to cope with a personal drug or alcohol problem vary widely, with the largest percentage saying they looked to an outsider, such as a minister or psychologist, for help. For many, as for a Pennsylvania FP, "abstinence is the only thing that works." Alcoholics Anonymous has worked for some, while others have tried everything from meditation to self-hypnosis.

The fact remains, however, that the majority of surveyed physicians don't consider overuse of alcohol a problem, either for themselves (only three out of 100 admit to overuse) or for their families. Fewer than four in 100 respondents believe their spouses have an alcohol problem, while only 1 percent say their children drink too much. Yet the National Clearinghouse for Alcohol Information estimates that almost four American adults in 10 who drink have a drinking problem; and the Department of Health, Education, and Welfare estimates that 3 million teen-agers, or more than 10 percent of the nation's teen population, are problem drinkers. It's difficult to believe that doctors and their families are this different from the general population.

How, then, do you explain the contradiction between national statistics and the surveyed doctors' perception of their own alcohol use? Again, it's that problem of facing up to realities. Some physicians clearly don't believe that their alcohol consumption presents a serious threat to their personal or professional lives. An Ohio GP who describes himself as a moderate drinker who occasionally overdoes it admits that he doesn't even try to curb the binges. He claims they're a better answer to his problems than some other solutions. A Florida FL sums up the feeling of the pro-alcohol forces when he says, "I don't see this as a problem. Booze is good."

Other doctors are apparently fooling themselves about the extent of their involvement with booze. A South Dakota FP says he overuses alcohol but adds, "I never drink when I'm working." A Pennsylvania pediatrician says he solved his alcohol-abuse problem by "drinking only low-alcohol beverages like beer." And an Illinois gynecologist claims "periodic total abstinence" solved his drinking problem. All these "solutions," according to various national studies, are considered red flags in the diagnosis of alcoholism.

Still another group of survey respondents think they may have a problem, but they're really not sure. "My wife and I both drink every day," says an Arkansas OBG specialist. "We rarely get to the point that we regret it, but I feel we may have become dependent on it." A Georgia FP writes: "I'm never really drunk, but it's become a habit. It bothers me."

Dr. Edward W. Lehman, chairman of the sociology department at New York University and a consultant for a recent American Academy of Family Physicians life-style survey, lends credence to the theory that many doctors may be reluctant to admit, to others or themselves, that they have a problem with drugs or alcohol. "Because doctors who are impaired by some type of chemical dependence face the risk of losing their licenses and because there's such a tremendous stigma attached to alcoholism and drug abuse, they may avoid coming to grips with this type of problem," Lehman says. "Even on an anonymous survey, it's possible that doctors will hedge their answers—perhaps subconsciously—for fear of being found out." Indeed, a doctor who has reached the point of physical or psychological dependence on drugs or alcohol probably isn't the most likely type to answer intimate survey questions about his personal life-style in the first place.

This reluctance to admit drug or alcohol overuse when it exists compounds the problem of the impaired physician. There are a number of programs available for the identification and treatment of impaired doctors. But as the AMA has noted in a study of the subject, no program will be completely successful until the doctors themselves approach the problem seriously and recognize that they have a problem.

"Alcoholic doctors are masters of manipulation," said a physician who is head of a hospital in a small city in New York State. "We try to police them, but they're so damned congenial and convincing." He explained that a doctor who is an alcoholic learns to deal with his needs skillfully so as to hide his condition from peers and patients.

"The trouble is their patients love them because they're so affable. The drinking makes them relaxed and happy. A slap on the back, a pat on the cheek, everyone is charmed. It's difficult to catch him because he drinks privately, of course, and is rarely, if ever, falling down drunk."

Then how do his fellow physicians detect his dependency? I asked. "It's usually the nursing staff who notice an erratic pattern. He may have mood swings or be hard to reach. Or he just doesn't show up when he's supposed to. The nurses

notice inappropriate reactions to situations and they report
it. It's still tough for us to prove even though we suspect.
For instance, a nurse reported she smelled liquor on the
breath of an attending physician in the emergency room.
When we confronted him, he laughed it off. 'I just had a
drink before I got the emergency call. Don't you guys ever
take a few drinks?' "

As the interview went on, he explained that in a small
community, a doctor's drinking is easier to notice. "He
gets stopped a few times for drunken driving and we find
out from the police, though they rarely arrest him. You
know, 'Just a warning, doc.' So we know to keep an eye on
him."

"The trouble is the alcoholic physician has ten times the
denial ability of the average drunk. He has an absolute inability to recognize weaknesses within himself. And he hates
to be treated by another doctor, which constitutes another
problem. Physicians are extremely uncomfortable treating
ill peers, especially if they are suffering from a socially dis-
tasteful ailment that reflects on the profession. As a result,
an alcoholic or addicted doctor who denies his affliction finds
his denial is eagerly supported by his peers who are only too
relieved and happy to accept it."

When the question arose, "How do you catch an alcoholic doctor in the act unless you find him reeling around
the O.R. or tippling in the corridors?" the doctor laughed
as he said, "Strangely enough, we once caught a suspected
alcoholic physician in just that way. He had a hospitalized
alcoholic patient who became uncontrollable and insisted
he must leave the hospital to get a drink. The distraught
doctor, intent on keeping his very ill patient in bed, dug into
his own pocket without thinking and pulled out a few little
bottles of vodka, those individual portions you get on
planes. So we really caught him with the goods.

"It's usually not that simple to get evidence of a doctor's
drinking. Unfortunately, we usually have to wait until he

commits some horrendous blunder before we can throw him off the staff.

"And another obstacle," he added, "his dismissal has to be okayed by the hospital board of trustees, and their attitude toward alcoholism is, well, accepting."

"You mean," I asked, "there are some drinkers on the board, too?"

He smiled ruefully. "Unfortunately, often."

So the difficulty of dealing with an impaired physician is complicated not by rules or laws, but by the motivations and emotions of all those involved.

First, we have the transgressor, whose intelligence enables him to cunningly hide his behavior and whose narcissism prevents him from facing up to his failure.

Second, we have the adulatory public, which finds it hard to recognize or even consider any sign of drugs or drink in men they regard as gods.

Third, we have the medical profession, which has a long history of arrogance that causes them to rebuff all accusations of error or weakness.

Fourth, we have the hospital administrators, who are more concerned with the treatment of doctors than of the patients. Unfortunately, the economics of running a hospital requires a health-care executive to view doctors as patient-getters rather than healers. In other words, active physicians bring in patients. Therefore, hospital management is loath to unload a source of income, and dismissing an alcoholic or addicted doctor who fills hospital beds is something they find many rationalizations to avoid.

Probably the most bizarre incident of impaired physicians whose aberrant behavior was ignored by their fellow physicians as well as the hospital administration was the case of the Marcus twins, Stuart and Cyril, both prominent gynecologists who worked in the prestigious New York Hospital. In July 1975, their bodies were found in their New York apartment. It was an absolute horror scene that shocked even the cynical New York police who found them. The place was unbelievably filthy, with rotting food and human waste all over the floors and vials of drugs everywhere. It presented a picture of the most utter degradation of two men whose lives had been filled with brilliant promise. The New York medical examiner said these two eminent physicians, only forty-five years old, had both died of acute drug withdrawal symptoms. The appalling fact was not only the waste of valuable brains and talent, but that both men had been allowed to reach this advanced stage of drug dependency and resultant deterioration without any action on the part of the hospital administration or their colleagues.

Matthew Lifflander, a lawyer, the director of the task force that investigated the case, was interviewed by Morley Safer on CBS's *60 Minutes* in a segment called "Doctor, Are You Hooked?" that was devoted to alcoholism and drug addiction in doctors.

> SAFER: How long had New York Hospital known about the Marcus twins?
> LIFFLANDER: Well, we found evidence that they were aware of some of the problems for as much as three years before they eventually terminated them, and that they were clearly aware of serious problems for fifteen months before the end.
> SAFER: Did they describe the symptoms of the illness?
> LIFFLANDER: They didn't, but other witnesses did. I mean—
> SAFER: Which were?
> LIFFLANDER: Well, one symptom was—quote—"The doctor was bouncing off the wall"—end quote—while attempting to perform surgery. On another occasion the doctor appeared in the emergency—in the emergency room because one of his patients was hemorrhaging. He kept that patient waiting for three hours. When the doctor arrived, the patient's husband said—took one look at him and said, "You're not going to touch my wife!"

ED WILLIAMS: I thought at first he was—he was drunk. That's what I—that was my impression.

SAFER: Ed Williams, the husband, is a New York radio announcer.

WILLIAMS: I say that because he was bobbing and weaving and he seemed incoherent and uncoordinated. I remember he had on a white suit. At one point he examined the blood on one of her napkins, and he tried to put his hand in his pocket. And you know how it is when a person seems to be drunk and they reach for the pocket a few times? Each time he reached, he smeared blood on his suit.

SAFER: He kept missing the pocket?

WILLIAMS: He kept missing the pocket. And at that—at—certainly at that point I was—it was clear in my mind that there was nothing I was going to allow him to do for my wife. So I called him aside, and I said, "Doctor, I don't believe that you're in any condition to—to administer any kind of medical help to anybody."

LIFFLANDER: A civilian was able to tell. I mean, the symptoms were pretty clear. The problem that this illustrates is that the medical profession is taking care of itself before it's taking care of its patients when faced with an impaired physician.

SAFER: What you're saying was that no one in New York Hospital in a period of from fifteen months to three years was willing to blow the whistle?

LIFFLANDER: Absolutely not.

SAFER: Is there something criminal in that?

LIFFLANDER: No, unfortunately, it's not criminal. It may be immoral, by my standards and by yours, but by the standards of the medical profession I think that they felt that we were imposing by asking some of these questions that you're asking.*

The medical profession is only now starting to face up to the sickness within its ranks. The American Medical Association, which would never before admit to anything that damaged the doctor's superior, pristine image, now encourages physicians to open up on the subject of the impaired physician. It holds regular conferences on how to break through the barriers that all addicts and alcoholics place between themselves and society.

In August 1974, a group of recovered alcoholic doctors called Doctors in AA (Alcoholics Anonymous) held their twenty-fifth annual weekend convention in Chicago. There are several hospitals and rehabilitation facilities, in New York, Pennsylvania, Minnesota, Illinois, and Georgia, that do special treatment for the alcoholic physician. The De Paul Rehabilitation Hospital in Milwaukee specializes in the care of alcoholic and addicted physicians and is run by Dr. Roland Herrington, a former alcoholic and drug addict.

Meanwhile, back in the home, the doctor's wife is witnessing or participating in the deterioration of her husband and is going through hell. She entered the marriage with love, hope, and the belief that as the wife of a physician she would spend her life securely with a strong, respected, and admirable husband and father of her children. Now suddenly this once strong figure has disintegrated into a depressed, devious, and often incoherent person who is unable to fulfill professional as well as familial responsibilities. She is scared, bewildered, desperate, and doesn't know where to turn for help.

The Menninger study found that many of the wives of alcoholic and addicted doctors, in subtle ways, abetted and encouraged their husbands' continuing psychological difficulties. Some actually joined their husbands and became addicts, and several were heavy drinkers. They also found that one aspect of the physician-addict's personality was a dependency on the emotional support of marriage, even though they were all spectacularly unsuccessful in performing the culturally patterned role of husbands.

As reported in the Menninger Foundation study:

> Only three of our twenty-four married patients appeared
> to have realized a relatively stable marital adjustment; the
> other twenty-one manifested heterosexual incompatibility,
> at least with the women they were somehow motivated to
> marry. In six marriages, violent conflicts included physical
> assault. Three patients were exaggeratedly dependent and
> deliberately overdemanding of their wives. Two patients
> retained dependent relationships with their natural
> mothers. Ten presented case histories of severe overt sexual
> incapacity. Several others, while denying premature ejac-
> ulations and impotence, did confess to episodes of prom-
> iscuity. A major number of the wives were frigid or
> promiscuous. Even though their wives could never really
> meet the unrealistic expectations and demands of the pa-
> tients, it is striking that they, nevertheless, remained mar-
> ried. The two patients who divorced promptly remarried.

Many doctors' wives are unwilling to break up their marriages no matter how intense the abuse because an unknown
future is often more frightening than a miserable present.
Often the husband's ability to hide his addiction and the
skill of his denial techniques lull her into accepting his
version of the facts and attributing his erratic behavior to
overwork or male menopause. She may well choose to
overlook or misinterpret the cause of his aberrant actions
because it suits her needs. It is very difficult to admit that
your once respected, loved husband is a junky or a drunk.
You are embarrassed, humiliated, ashamed, and, worst of
all, guilty. How did this happen? Why didn't you see it coming and stop it? How have you failed him? Why couldn't
you provide him with the strength to withstand whatever
devils tortured him? And worst of all, there is the nagging
suspicion that he is taking drugs or alcohol to escape from
you. Certain wives continue to perpetuate the denial; some
crack under the strain themselves; others take whatever

actions they feel are necessary for the protection of themselves and their children.

Edith and Charles met in the army. She was a nurse and he a doctor, and there was instant attraction. Edith was strong, opinionated, and a colorful activisit. Charles was a placid man who liked to watch the world go by and he enjoyed Edith as a spectator sport. They were married while still in uniform.

After the war, they both wanted a house, family, and a settled life. Charles took a job as assistant to an internist in a very busy city practice and set up a weekend practice of his own in a specially built office wing of the house they bought in a new suburb. First came Evelyn, then Mark, and then Arthur, and within five years Charles found himself with a family, a mortgage, and a hectic schedule that kept him in a state of exhaustion. Finally, when his own practice had developed sufficiently, he gave up the city job and now felt he had fulfilled his life's dream by being GP in a fine suburban community where he would be called upon and needed for the rest of his life.

Edith had become a political power in the community and she kept Charles and herself busy with social-cum-political commitments for all their free time. Wherever there was a protest movement, Edith would be found leading the marchers. All her friends admired and envied her. She enjoyed a prestigious position in the community as an activist and a doctor's wife, had a lovely income and luxurious life-style, a nice husband, and bright kids. What more could a woman want?

Charles began to find the hectic home atmosphere wearing. The children, reared in Edith's image, were noisy, aggressive, and assertive, and they would barge into his office and interrupt his little free time. He found himself uncomfortable with their questions and inadequate to cope with their problems. Once he even wondered if he was really cut out to be a father but dismissed the thought hurriedly in horror.

By the time Charles was forty-five, most of his patients had been with him for years and his practice was comfortable, constant, and unchallenging; any unusual conditions or ailments were dispatched to big-city specialists. Sometimes he tried to catch Edith for a moment between her commitments to talk about the dreams they had about doing something meaningful in medicine to help mankind. One evening, he noticed a flyer of Edith's announcing a major fund-raising drive to help the impoverished mining families in Appalachia who were in dire need of food, clothing, and health care. Suddenly, the idea hit him and he dashed into the kitchen where Edith was preparing dinner: "Let's move to Virginia," he said excitedly. "You're a nurse, I'm a doctor, we could really help people who needed us. I'd feel I was doing something important, and it would be good for the kids, too . . ." He stopped when he saw the horrified expression on Edith's face. "Are you mad? Give up this great practice and life and move to that hellhole?"

"I thought you wanted to correct injustice whenever you saw it, that's what you always said you were dedicating your life to," said Charles. "Well, now's your chance to really make an important contribution."

Edith eyed him scornfully. "You're nuts. I help the people enough. I raise money for them and fight for legislation. That doesn't mean I have to live with them!"

A few days later, Charles volunteered his services to a ghetto clinic in a neighboring community and began to work weekends and evenings and come home utterly exhausted. Often keyed up and weary, he found he could not always get to sleep, so he took some barbiturates. When he felt foggy and groggy the next day, he took amphetamines to keep him going. Soon, he began to take ten, then twenty, then more pills every day. Edith noticed the change in his behavior and the violent mood swings from exhilaration one moment to deep depression the next. One day, one of Charles's patients stopped Edith on the street to inquire after the doctor's health; she was concerned about him because he had been unable to remember her name on her last visit, and she had been his patient for ten years.

Another wife might have attributed this lapse to exhaustion, but Edith was a nurse and had seen cases of drug addiction. She began a systematic search of the house and office and was appalled to discover caches of pills everywhere—in Charles's tie drawer, buried under shirts, in his shaving kit. The moment he walked in the door that evening, she confronted him head-on, in typical no-nonsense Edith fashion. "You're a drug addict and you'd better go for help, buster." Of course, Charles denied her allegation, but Edith would have none of his excuses. Day after day, she harangued him to go for therapy. "I'm not going to allow you to ruin my life and the children's lives by staying with an addict. Either you go for help or out you go."

Within months, Edith filed for divorce. Fortunately, Charles met a kindly, warmhearted woman with whom he lived for a while and then married, after putting himself into therapy to break his habit.

Edith was a strong-minded independent woman with her own profession; she could leave a husband with whom she found life untenable because she had valid aternatives, as did this doctor's wife of thirty-one years whose comments came to *Medical/Mrs.* on the bottom line of her survey form:

As a professional person also, envisioned was partnership in complementary roles especially after "mothering days" lessened. My husband gradually took on the "God" syndrome but worst of all was the social drinking increased to alcoholism. We are now in process of divorce as he no longer could be congenial with me and left the house. He

was in constant denial of his "problem" and his physician
could not help either.

But what about the woman who does not have these resources and is bewildered by the terrifying strange twist her
life has taken? Her choices are to stay and try to help him,
or turn to drugs or alcohol for her own support.

Drug use and drunkenness are often attributed to doctors'
wives; the picture of idle, sulky, discontented women re-
sorting to drugs and liquor to assuage their intense boredom
is a popular conception. Although endless studies are now
coming out in medical journals and the popular media on
alcoholism and addiction in physicians, nothing definitive
has been done on their wives. However, throughout the
literature on medical marriages, statements on alcoholism
and addiction of wives crop up.

A study that appeared in the *Texas State Journal of
Medicine* called "The Doctor and His Marriage" described
a clinical observation of twenty-five physicians' wives in a
private psychiatric hospital as contrasted with twenty-five
married women patients of similar ages. These significant
statistics emerged: Out of the twenty-five doctors' wives,
eight had drinking problems, ten used barbiturates or amphetamines, and three used narcotics. In the non-doctors'
wives group, only two women used alcohol, one barbiturates, and none narcotics. In an article called "Psychiatric
Illness in the Physician's Wife" that appeared in the *American Journal of Psychiatry*, it was noted that among fifty
doctors' wives hospitalized at the Institute for Living, drug
addiction was common.

All these numbers are easy to analyze: Doctors' wives in
emotional difficulty will resort to the same sources of relief
as their husbands for the same reasons—accessibility and
familiarity. To most of us, pills and medication are regarded
with awe and a bit of fear; we read the bottles and the
pharmaceutical caveats "Available by prescription only,"

"This prescription CANNOT be refilled," and we take them only upon the advice of our physicians. But in a medical household, drugs are always around in bulk and are dispensed like candy. The doctor's bag is filled with all those samples from the pharmaceutical companies, his medicine cabinet is lined with little white boxes of free pills. Whenever a member of the family reports any discomfort, physical or emotional, the doctor has a pill handy to make the trouble go away.

As a woman who is the daughter of a doctor and now the wife of one explained, "There were always lots of pills around the house. When I want to lose weight, my husband gives me Dexedrine. Then I get so hopped up at first that I can't sleep, so he gives me Valium. He's always giving us a pill for this and that; we take them for granted. But drugs are for relief, aren't they? Addiction?—of course not. We're a doctor's family, we know better."

VIII

The Rude Awakening:
Self-Actualization and
the Women's Movement

"And what do YOU do?" The question irritated the doctor's wife, who was once again faced with that now commonplace cocktail party query. "I'm a housewife," she said defensively.

Time was when no one asked a woman what she did. The assumption was, if she was married, that she was a mother and housewife and you knew what she did all day, so why bother asking and risk being hit with a boring barrage of minutiae about toilet training and the PTA? You asked a man what he did because his career was an indication of the person and enabled you to make an instant evaluation of his rating on your "worth talking to" barometer. But these days, thanks to the women's movement, distaffs are defecting from the ranks of homemakers and working on equal levels with men. Which means freedom for those wives who want to break out of the home ties and follow careers or professions, and guilt for the women who opt to stay home.

For a majority of doctors' wives, this new challenge has brought unexpected pain and bewilderment. Fifty-four percent of doctors' wives who responded to the *Medical/Mrs.* "Myth vs. Reality" survey said that they married doctors because the "Image conveyed security and happiness and pride." Sixty-seven percent felt they had achieved a "Good marriage . . . everywoman's dream." In effect they had it made, the queen of the community, the doctor's wife. And now what they had perceived as social success is in ashes. They had been trading on their spouses' position for social status which had always been the acceptable social yard-stick—you are who you marry—and now suddenly they are out there naked, totally on their own. "What do *you* do?" means "Who are you?" not "Who is your husband?"

Most doctors' wives live derivative existences. If you have any problem with that statement, read a book called *How to Be a Doctor's Wife Without Really Dying*, written by Marguerite Hurrey Wolf. The entire book, described as "humorous," is devoted to, quoting the book jacket, the author's "career" as a doctor's wife who "believes that the enjoyment of the multifaceted life of a doctor's wife calls for endurance part of the time, a profound respect for the medical profession at all times, and a sense of humor that is on call at all hours." Can you imagine any other woman considering her husband's profession as the cornerstone of her identity? Or, say, a woman writing a "humorous" book about her experiences as, for instance, the wife of a plumber maybe called *How to Be a Plumber's Wife*, or *Twenty Years Down the Drain*.

In her book, Mrs. Wolf devotes twenty-five chapters to the pleasures and problems of being married to a doctor. She does give recognition to the changing role of the doctor's wife since the thirty years ago when she first entered the holy bonds of medical matrimony.

"What the doctor's wife used to be was a pair of hands and emotional support. Now she is a mind." She goes on to point out that the requirements of a doctor's wife in helping with patients has changed due to new technologies and methods of practicing medicine. But she has not been programmed out of her role as a doctor's wife, merely shifted positions a bit. "Whereas she used to be active at her husband's elbow or, if she was a town or city wife, hospital oriented in terms of auxiliary work, she is now more community oriented . . . involved in mental health, planned parenthoods."

The fact is that Mrs. Wolf and thousands like her had no identity problem. They knew who they were, were proud of it, and worked at it—they were "doctors' wives" dedicated to supplementing their husbands as guardians of the public health. Society applauded them, the other ladies of the community respected and envied them. They had position, mission, and money. But all of a sudden, it's changed. Today you have to be somebody, not married to somebody, and the old passalong status deal has lost its validity.

Thousands of doctors' wives have stayed in their derivative roles. The American Medical Association Auxiliary has a national membership of eighty thousand who work hard at their careers of being full-time doctors' wives and outwardly seem content. But thousands more are coming out of the closet and pursuing means of independent self-fulfillment. "I'm sick of being 'Mrs. Doctor Smith,'" writes one wife. "I have no identity and my husband enjoys that fact." According to psychiatrist Harold Marcus: "Doctors' wives more than any other group must make independent lives for themselves. They must have their own interests and careers so that they are not totally dependent upon their husbands to fill emotional needs." There is a major highly charged rift in the ranks of doctors' wives today between the "Mrs. Doctors" and the "I am me" groups, but both sides have one factor in common: No matter which route they follow, it will be a bit tougher just because they are doctors' wives.

When I was on the *Phil Donahue Show* in June 1979 for a special program devoted to medical marriages and the unhappiness uncovered in the *Medical/Mrs.* survey, the audience was all AMA Auxiliarians. Their obviously well-choreographed homogeneity on the issue of the utter joys of being married to doctors was clear evidence of their feeling the need to close ranks against attacks. Any suggestion of a situation that could cause difficulty in a medical marriage was rebutted with such ferocious pollyannaism that it became ludicrous. Clearly they are being threatened by incursions into the solid state of status previously enjoyed and coveted during those prefeminist years. And they don't like it.

When Phyllis Savin, wife of Santa Barbara surgeon Max Savin, who has been a student of Dr. Philip Barrata in his course given at the University of California in San Diego titled "Physician's Wife—No Bed of Roses," spoke softly of the emotional deprivation she had been subjected to, the failures of her expectations in the marriage because of her husband's commitment to his patients and practice, the audience's outcry was so spontaneous and similar as to seem orchestrated. Of course, a representative of the office of public relations of the AMA was there; she had brought the audience, but not without stipulations. The threat to the doctor's wife image was one they take seriously, and they resorted to strong measures to get what they saw as "their side" heard. When the producer of the show approached with the request for an audience of doctors' wives, the AMA responded with a demand. Yes, they would fill the hall, but only if "their representative" would also appear on the dais with Dr. Barrata and Mrs. Savin. They knew Mrs. Savin was a doctor's wife, but apparently not in good standing in the opinion of the AMA. How could she be? She was unhappy with her role, and in their eyes this represents heresy. It also represents risk, since the AMA membership and thus financial position is affected by commitment to the cause of protecting the exalted position of the doctor. Any criticism of the profession, or indications that doctors are less than paragons, is met with powerful AMA resistance.

According to a major editorial in the AMA Auxiliary publication following the Donahue show they "negotiated beforehand to have Auxiliary member Pat Walker of Missouri on the stage to tell the other side of the medical spouse story." The fact that they acknowledge that there is another side indicates a visible crack in their previously smug position of implacable rectitude.

The choice of spokeswoman was an indication of the AMA's simplistic approach to patrolling against opposition. For Pat Walker (Mrs. William, whose husband is president of the Greene County Missouri Medical Society) is a woman of aggressive cheerfulness with an inflexibly sunny disposition and determined single-mindedness in her view of the perfection of her existence as "the doctor's wife." Her references to "our practice" and when "we took in a partner" only pointed up the wife's immersion in her husband's career that the AMA sees as idyllic. Every statement from Mrs. Savin or Dr. Barrata that alluded to familial failures in a medical marriage or a desire for parity in the relationship was parried with if not interrupted by Mrs. Walker's staunch refutation. The audience reacted with what the AMA publication reported as a "spirited defense of medical marriages . . . Donahue intended to give medical wives a chance to air their grievances . . . two hundred doctor's wives, all members of the AMA Auxiliary from five midwestern states, crowded the WGN TV studio in Chicago and parried Donahue's every thrust." What came through was a vehemently defensive denial of any negatives in medical marriages and an unrealistic twenty-four-hours-of-joy attitude that raised more questions than it answered. The TV audience saw a group of women aided and abetted by a powerful organization under whose direction they were fighting to preserve a status status quo that is no longer relevant to the sensibilities of today's women.

"For the past ten years," said Dr. Barrata, "I have never been without a doctor's wife in my private psychiatric practice. It has to do with rising expectations. Doctors' wives are asking questions they wouldn't dream of asking years ago." The totally derivative existence formerly demanded of a doctor's wife is no longer seen as acceptable by all women or by society. The feminist movement has pointed out the importance of independent self-esteem, a life approach previously denied to women by themselves or by established social parameters. Can you see any woman today, in this era of raised consciousness, accepting this statement which concluded an article entitled "The Doctor's Image" written in 1969 by clinical psychologist Dr. Peter J. Hampton?

> It is only as the doctor's wife finds herself in her husband's dedicated purpose for living that she can truly understand and accept him in his many images. A woman must be many things to her doctor husband. She must be his wife and in a sense his mother; she must be his companion and his confidante; she must be his sweetheart and his mistress. Thus, says Rembrandt, the great painter, can she become the many in one of her husband so that he will not deviate his affiliation and design from her.
>
> Whether she is the wife of an obstetrician or a pediatrician, an internist or a general practitioner, a surgeon or a neurologist, she must dedicate herself to her doctor husband if she is to find herself intellectually, socially, emotionally and physically. A big order? Yes! But what an exciting one. The doctor stands on a pedestal in our culture. And so does the doctor's wife. And this is a place well deserved by both because they've earned it.

Building a life solely upon the career of one's husband is an alien concept to most contemporary women. But to the eighty thousand members of the AMA Auxiliaries, life is still a round of activities dedicated to medical-related goals and programs. As they see it, according to Mrs. Ben Johnson, president of the national organization, marriage to a doctor is "meant to be a life of service," and the auxiliary wives are "committed to help physicians provide the best possible medical care." Their role is to be supportive adjuncts of their husbands, and even their so-called independent hours are spent in pursuits reflective of their husbands' profession. After years of acceptance, they have a tremendous emotional investment in this status-by-osmosis position, and the sudden questioning of its validity is seen as virtually life-threatening.

This letter from a San Diego doctor's wife, sent to *Medical/Mrs.* and to the *San Diego Physician* magazine, is a perfect extension of the AMA stand on "spirited defense of medical marriages." The AMA, by running articles from time to time on marital problems, is at least willing to admit that difficulties can be created by pulls of the profession. Mrs. Peterson is so "spirited" in her defense that she denies the existence of any flaws in her life and paints a picture of an idyllic perfection that could come only from a marriage between Barbie and Ken dolls. As a final testimonial to the marvelous living conditions offered by the privilege of being married to a doctor, she places any blame for possible discontent solely on the head of the "dumb" wife.

Dear Sirs:

In response to an article from your magazine on doctors unhappy wives, carried by the *New York Times* and subsequent newspapers throughout the country, I'd like to make a comment.

I am disappointed that you published only the negative responses of doctors' wives. I have always been under the impression that a positive attitude was the key to success.

America has positive ideals. However, some of our brain-washers in the government and in the news media are undermining these ideals. Consequently, they are tearing down the status of many good things in the United States including the status of the doctor.

If you are going to publish comments of unhappy doctors wives, you should give the "happy doctors wives" equal time.

I've been married to a Family Physician and Surgeon for fourteen years with no room to complain! My husband has a heavy practice which he really cares about and his patients love him. He is on the medical staff of San Diego's Juvenile Hall which he visits daily and is on call twenty-four hours a day. He is Chief of Staff of one of our community hospitals and is on the staff of every hospital within a thirty-five-mile radius, which means added responsibilities and meetings. Every doctor must attend Continuing Medical Education classes in order to keep his license to practice medicine active and my husband is no exception.

With this schedule one might think he'd be exhausted and it's no wonder that he has no time for his family. WRONG! This doctor happens to get everyone in the house up in the morning and take the kids to school on his way to the hospitals. After seeing morning patients he takes a two hour lunch break so he can have time to spend at Juvenile Hall. More often than not he has no time to eat, yet he will take the time to go to the central library, downtown, to pick up records and books on an opera for his eleven-year-old Girl Scout and still gets back to the office for afternoon patients. Often he stops at a hospital or nursing home on his way home from the office. Many times I have been running with our kids all day and don't have dinner ready and he will suggest that we all relax and eat out.

He is the Congregational Chairman and Chairman of the Board of our church and seldom misses a Sunday service. Every Wednesday night we have Bible Study in our home for our church members. He wouldn't think of missing the Padre ballgame when they're in town and of course he takes one of his kids or myself with him. If there's a school meeting, we go together.

On Thursday afternoon, his day off, he has a tennis lesson. He says that he has to "keep in shape" so neither of his two teenage sons will beat him at the game.

I must mention our enjoyment of the theatre, the skiing trips with the kids, our biannual family vacations and the occasional weekend we get away by ourselves.

He gets so involved in projects that I take on that he is my enthusiasm. He gives me the desire to do my best.

He's no god. He's just a good American doctor that is hard working and conscientious. A man who thinks the world of his wife and kids.

I really think you "goofed" when you published the negative comments from unhappy doctors wives because most of the doctors' families I know are similar to ours.

Every doctor's wife I know is spoiled rotten! Most of us live in multi-figured costing homes with housekeeping help, swimming pools, nice cars, a beautiful family and a guy who really loves us. How dumb can some wives be not to be able to handle that!

It sounds to me like those wives who married for "prestige, security, happiness, pride and the satisfaction of performing as a loyal helpmate to a man of service" should have married for love and let the rest of it all follow!

I am convinced that any doctor that doesn't have time for his family doesn't want to take time. Perhaps his wife should look at herself and find the reason why!

Respectfully,

Sally Peterson
A doctor's happy wife!

It is difficult for the nonmedical wife to understand the extent of identification and absorption a medical spouse has with her husband's career. When Pat Walker mentioned that life would now be much easier because "we now have an associate to cover for us so that we'll have more free time," that did not mean that she worked actively in his practice. She doesn't. It was merely doctor's wife patois; the involvement with his profession is so consummate that the plural pronoun is always used. The first exposure I had to this phenomenon was in a focus group that we used to market-test the viability of *Medical/Mrs.* before it was launched. A focus group is a meeting of people who constitute a microcosm of the market you intend to reach. The purpose of our focus group was to learn if doctors' wives are, in fact, an affinity group with related lines of thinking, and if so, what subjects would interest them. We suspected a degree of association with their husbands' profession but were startled to learn the extent. When asked what sorts of articles would be welcome in "their" magazine, they answered, "articles about doctors' hobbies" and "where doctors go on vacation." They were not interested in what *people* did for hobbies or went on vacation—just *doctors.* When we asked with whom they customarily socialize, who were their friends, physicians predominated. The final touch was the ophthalmic surgeon's wife who rose to leave before the meeting was over with this apology, "I'm sorry, I must go now. I have to be up early tomorrow because we're operating."

Identification with her husband's profession starts early in the marriage, as seen in this piece by doctor's wife Georgene Simon Dreishpoon that appeared in the January/ February 1978 issue of *Medical/Mrs.*:

Smile, You're the Doctor's Wife

An essential ingredient of being a successful doctor is a sense of humor. If you are a doctor's wife . . . double the recipe!

I vividly remember entering solo practice some 23 years ago. We elected to have our home and office together for practical purposes; practical meant that the wife would act as nurse, answering service, cook, housekeeper, gardener, and mother of two infants. In my spare time, I was to look and act like Marilyn Monroe.

We were beset by the usual anxieties. Where will the patients come from and will they come? Can we set up an efficient office on a shoestring budget? Will we make a living?

Advice was free flowing from a family of fellow professionals. A sample from my father, a general surgeon, was, "If your husband has a patient referred: 1—get him in immediately; 2—lock him in the waiting room, 3—keep him there until you have tracked down the doctor and connected him with the patient." He claimed that during his first six months of practice, it was so slow that he went around to the local drugstore to call his office. He wanted to make sure the phone was working. This story did wonders for bolstering our security.

Three days before our "grand opening," attired in old jeans and shirts, we labored to ready our office. The shingle bearing our name had gone up proudly, with number one priority. I had just finished hanging a collection of signs that my husband felt were essential. The bathroom was designated LAVATORY and the front door displayed RING BELL/WALK IN and PLEASE REMOVE RUBBERS.

As I stood back to admire our newly adorned front door, a man suddenly approached me. He was frantically looking for a doctor. He had been stung by a bee, and momentarily expected to go into anaphylactic shock. I ran to the rear of the house to uncover the doctor from a roll of carpeting he was attempting to lay. Despite his two-day growth of beard, blue jean attire and healthy perspiration, professional duty prevailed. He hastened to the man's call. I wish that a camera had recorded the facial expression on our bee-bitten friend. He took one look at my husband and said, "Are you the doctor?" My healer of men, trying to sound professional, said, "Yes, Sir." The man glanced at our prominent new white couch in the waiting room and timidly asked, "A psychiatrist?" My husband informed him that he was an obstetrician. With that reply, a projectile vomiting ensued, spurting from the man to the wall of our newly papered waiting room. We were launched into practice!

One week later, a referred patient appeared unexpectedly at the office door. Following my father's advice, I locked her in the waiting room with the assurance that the doctor would be with her shortly. As luck would have it, the doctor had chosen this time to participate in a set or two of tennis. He had taken our only car and there was no phone at the court. I was frantically considering my options when my father arrived on the scene. Since it was his advice that I was following, he volunteered to fetch his errant son-in-law. My husband later related that father had appeared at the court behind the wheel of his large grey Cadillac. As my husband reached for an overhead smash, there was a shrill whistle, followed by "Irving, you have a patient in the waiting room. Get home!" Irving's partner, a dignified lawyer of the community, commented, "Irving, you sure have a fancy messenger boy."

One morning, as I was stuffing cereal into the mouth of the baby, I answered a phone call which jolted me into awareness. "Is this Dr. Dreishpoon's office?" a voice asked. "This is the chairman of the Medical Ethics Committee." He continued, "Does your husband have a sign posted on his front door stating PLEASE REMOVE RUBBERS?" I said "Yes," thinking this was a serious matter. He continued, "The committee feels that this sign is highly unethical for an obstetrician's office." With a roar of laughter, he identified himself, wished us good luck, and hung up. That evening there was a lengthy discussion as to whether the sign should be removed or replaced with PLEASE REMOVE YOUR GALOSHES.

With the passing of the years, the expectations of our youth have been happily realized. It has been my fortune to share two generations of doctors' stories. Without doubt, the advice received from the first generation is still the best, "Keep Smiling."

All right, you say, this was twenty-five years ago. Would this two-people-living-one-life approach be feasible in today's climate of feminine self-actualization? Here is an article received from a young doctor's wife, Rose-Ellen Benkel, which appeared in the January/February 1979 issue:

The Transformation

I supported my husband through his final year of medical school. We had planned it that way, so that we could be married.

Upon graduation, my husband assumed the role of breadwinner, and I of mother-to-be. Throughout his training we regarded the hospital as his home away from home, and our source of steady income. At the beginning of his final year of residency, we became increasingly aware of the fact that July would be upon us, and the institution that was so vital to our lives for the last three years, our final hold on the security that all perpetual students seem to have, was going to take a back seat to reality.

Where to begin? Whom does one contact? What does one do? How does medical school, internship, and residency prepare you to begin your life in the field of your choice? It doesn't!

And that's the beginning of a long chain of events that transformed my husband from a student, to a doctor, to a man.

The transformation didn't take very long. Over the winter we decided, after much deliberation, that the most alluring possibility was to open our own practice. By spring we had secured a walk-in basement apartment. Despite the fact that there was nothing in there besides the four walls and a concrete floor, we could see visions of our shining new office. Our contractors, as it turned out, were also our landlords. And so, after several evenings of haggling over coffee, they decided that having a doctor's office in their house would be a considerable asset, and began to build it for one-third its real worth. A loan from the bank for accessories, and we were on our way.

We watched our office being built, with all the anxieties that go along with building and contractors. We prayed it would be ready by July, and between prayers, we ran around making arrangements for furniture, equipment, carpet, paneling, shades for the windows, wallpaper, and other such expensive goodies.

While my husband roamed the neighborhood introducing himself to doctors and pharmacies alike, I stuffed envelopes with announcements for the coming of his office and his business cards.

Through the weeks that followed, he read everything he could get his hands on, questioned everyone he knew, and inquired into every aspect of running an office.

On July 1, 1977, I drove Dr. Mark Benkel to our finished product. Outside the door was his spanking-new white shingle with black lettering hanging on a post that took two hours to select, and inside the office was the finished physician that took eleven years to make.

Obviously women like Mrs. Dreishpoon and Mrs. Benkel choose to pursue a derivative existence because it suits their needs and meets their goals. And the incursions of the women's movement have not disturbed them sufficiently to alter their direction. But thousands of other doctors' wives have reacted by becoming ashamed of their volunteer work in the hospitals and been driven into other areas of so-called self-fulfillment that are sometimes successful and sometimes dismal fiascoes. This column by me addressed itself to just this problem.

Yesterday I walked into the new boutique that opened in our town and was saddened to recognize the neophyte entrepreneur as the wonderful woman whom I had met in United Hospital last year when, as a member of the auxiliary, she helped me through a rough period during my father's operation.

Another defection from the ranks of valuable volunteers into the world of commerce. Is she another casualty of the misinterpretation of the women's movement wherein it is assumed that one is not a fulfilled person unless the value of her work is defined in cash? I ran into a lot of that when I taught a course for women at the University of Connecticut called "How to Start Your Own Business." I soon realized that many of the students really enjoyed their lives as wives, mothers and volunteer workers, but the necessity of answering that cocktail query "and what do YOU do?" with "I'm a housewife" had driven them into quests for commercial careers. But being in business is a consuming commitment replete with worries, tension and many anguished hours of "why am I doing this?" And rarely does it involve any great contribution to the human condition.

Volunteer work in hospitals, charities and political organizations is vitally needed and the achievements can be fulfillment enough, providing that the need to earn money is not a factor. I wistfully wished our boutique entrepreneur much luck. She was marvelously helpful to me and others at the hospital, but if success in business is important to her self-esteem (I know it's not the money in her case)—then I say "right on." But if she has been driven from an important and satisfying volunteer job to conform to some superficial social image as a "working woman," then I say it's a pity.

I know these women, because they were my students in a course on "How to Start Your Own Business" which I created for and taught at the University of Connecticut and later at Pace University. Since I have started and built three businesses, I felt I could help the legions of women who wanted to enter the world of commerce but were hampered by fears and ignorance. The course covered finance, sales promotion, and all other basic elements of which one must be knowlegeable in order to run a business. It was fairly comprehensive and included guest speakers from the banking community who explained how to handle the major difficulty of raising money.

I put a great deal of time into the lesson plan to ensure that these neophytes would learn how to cope with the exigencies that would surely face them. But it was I who learned. My assumption had been that the registrants had come to the class filled with motivation to break out of the shallow so-called woman's world previously assigned to them and to assert their individuality by starting an enterprise entirely on their own. I soon realized that the real impetus for going into business was not actually to start one but merely to say you were "working on the plans to start a business." It sounds so much better than "housewife" when you get the "what do you do" question. It was amazing to what ambitious extremes they let their minds go in blueprinting their future fantasy. Two women (doctors' wives) announced they intended to open a coffee bean store and wanted advice on procedures for national franchising of the operation! They attended three classes and then took off for South America on a buying-source scouting trip subsidized by their indulgent husbands, with the bland assumption that the entire trip would be tax deductible. From what?

With few exceptions, most of them sought an enterprise that would not encroach too heavily on tennis, bridge, and luncheon commitments. The popular consensus of the ideal was "a little mail order business." The name conjured up images of sitting in the basement opening envelopes filled with dollars, typing labels, and taking neat packages to the post office—all done in one's spare time. I explained to them that a "little mail order business" is just that, little and unprofitable, marginal at best. Mail order today is a vast, closely computerized industry where million-dollar volumes are commonplace and, in fact, necessary to survival. The next favorite was a shop, a boutique. In vain did I warn them of the realities of retailing, such as the fact that your body must be on the premises Saturdays, evenings, and other inconvenient times, and that you must be skilled in buying as well as selling in order to flourish. They saw a shop as a cozy social center where they would chat amiably with customers, show wares, and incidentally sell merchandise. The harsh facts of profits and losses and overhead did not cloud the rosy picture.

A goodly number of the students were wives of doctors. Two of them did go into a mail order business partnership and thus in a short time managed to lose money and break up a twenty-year friendship. Their concept of buying was to purchase merchandise from a manufacturer a little at a time to minimize their investment risk, which of course maximized their unit cost, since prices are based on quantity purchased. They then computed what they needed to cover costs and provide them with a reasonable profit and just marked up each piece accordingly. What they never bothered to do was comparison shop in order to learn the market prices of similar products. Needless to say, their overpriced offerings did not achieve any great volume, and that plus the split-responsibility resentments—Norma was in the Caribbean when the orders came in so Joan had to do all the shipping, and so on—began to cause arguments. I kept hearing how much they enjoyed being in business, how they felt they were made for it, and how could they have missed all these years of fun. They were stars at dinner and cocktail parties now; no longer just doctors' wives, they were modern, liberated women who were independent entrepreneurs. The new roles lasted until the money ran out and their husbands turned off the cash flow, at which time they quit and their true lack of purpose was exposed.

These women plus thousands of others truly enjoyed the reflected glory and easy life of Mrs. Doctor, but the women's movement has given them a case of feminist guilts. They shrink under the scorn of their grown daughters who liked having stay-at-home moms when they were tots but now view their mothers as spiritless drones. Caught between two generations of women's work ethics, they are understandably bewildered and angry. However, many wives of doctors have found the new climate of approval for working women has given them freedom to enter areas they longed to, but never before dared enter. And in so doing, they discovered feelings about themselves that are new and rejuvenating.

"I was the victim of a liberal arts education. I learned to love art, music, and literature, but I wasn't trained to work at anything." So says Florence Scherz, who's now a highly successful business woman.

Florence owns Nibbles, a gourmet food shop in Newton, Massachusetts, and she frequently caters cocktail parties, dinner parties, and other events. Recently, she began manufacturing two of her popular cheese spreads for national distribution. Florence also happens to be a psychiatrist's wife, a mother of three, and an ex-homemaker.

To hear her speak with such relaxed commercial expertise, it is staggering to realize that she started her business just four years ago . . . with absolutely no preparation or training. At that time, her youngest son was ready for nursery school, and she was ready for a change. Florence has neither an M.B.A. from Harvard nor a culinary certificate from the Cordon Bleu; all her "business training" took place in her own kitchen.

"I'd been home for fifteen years. I'd mastered entertaining, sewing, furniture refinishing, antiquing, painting, and pottery making. But now I wanted a paying profession or job," she says.

"While I was home raising my children, many of my friends were out advancing their careers. So by the time I was ready to work, they were all 'up there,' and I was not willing to start as a sales clerk," she adds.

Florence assessed her skills: food and entertaining were what she knew best. Throwing hundreds of lavish parties had given her valuable work experience.

"Everyone tried to talk me out of starting my own business," she recalls. "No bank would give me credit. My suppliers had to be paid in advance." So she financed that first venture with the help of her family.

"My original plan," says Florence, "was to have a continental charcuterie, a place where people could come to buy something to embroider their meals. I offered soups, pâtés, quiches, hors d'oeuvres, entrées, vegetables, and incredible European desserts." She did all the cooking herself and hired one employee to help with the sales.

How much money did she start out with? "Seven thousand dollars," replies Florence. "But I was undercapitalized. More businesses fail because of not enough capital than for any other reason. If I'd had seventy thousand dollars, I'd have had an easier time of it."

Her first Nibbles shop was in a converted garage on a poor street for a retail business. As Florence admits, "It was a leap of faith. But I was willing to take risks, and I wasn't willing to fail."

Within two years, her business grew by 200 percent. Once she had a proven track record, banks were willing to lend Florence money for expansion. An appreciative customer offered to rent her space in a desirable location, so she moved to larger quarters and hired six more employees.

Remember that for fifteen years Florence was always available to her husband and the children. "My husband is enormously critical of what I'm doing," says Florence. "He liked things better the way they were. But he also understands my needs. I enjoy what I'm doing and I need the dignity of feeling good about myself."

Two of Florence's three children say it's fun to have a mother with a shop. But her middle son, eleven-year-old Josh, says it "stinks" to have a mother who's always busy.

On the day that Florence gave us this interview, she was in the midst of hiring a new housekeeper. "When I was home," says Florence, "I didn't mind managing the house. But now that I'm working, I resent the housework. I'd burn out without good help," she said.

Her children seem to agree. They speak of one male housekeeper who stayed over a year. "He did model airplanes with us," explains Josh, "and that was OK. But without a housekeeper, it's hard on us."

"People tell me I look younger, happier, and more attractive since I've gone into business," says this woman who's been married half her life. However, she admits starting a retail business takes money, hard work, and a great deal of family cooperation.

When any wife goes back to work after years of being the fulcrum of the household, there are problems of adjustment within the family and the husband is expected to make many compromises. If he understands the deeply personal need that has driven his wife to the decision, he is willing to make the sacrifices for her sake. If they need the additional income, he is willing to make the sacrifices for the family's sake. But if he is a doctor, none of the above apply. This is an indiviual who has been made to feel that full-time service is his due. He has been accustomed in the hospital and his office to receive finger-snapping responses to his needs. After years of this conditioning, he finds it difficult to accept the inconveniences that are inevitable when his wife has gone out to work. Note how Florence Scherz's husband is "enormously critical" of what she is doing. He had been used to full-scale service where his needs and comforts came first; now suddenly another batch of needs has emerged to compete with his. In his column in *Medical/Mrs.*, Dr. Lawrence Hatterer advises women who decide to return to work after years of full-time homemaking to first discuss the decision with their husbands.

> He has to know how his and your life will be changed. How much change can he tolerate? What will he do to help? Are his and your sacrifices possible in the light of your previous life-style? His belief in your ability to carry out your plan and his good will are imperative. Many a physician has verbally encouraged his wife in a career, but the statements come from the head rather than the heart. Sitting down alone to a cold dinner, or one he removed

from the oven may not be as easy for him to face in fact
as in theory. Can he accept nights when *you* fall asleep
too early to make love because you are as exhausted as he
had been with his overprogrammed life? A shift in the
dominance-submission patterns between you must occur.
This will put your relationship to the acid test. Flexibility,
unselfishness and understanding will be required all
around.

Unfortunately, flexibility, unselfishness, and understanding are in short supply in the medical profession. Their training has created a self-image of king-of-the-hill with an
established elaborate support system consisting of varied
hospital personnel all subordinate to the physician, and
the office nurses and receptionists who protect and adore
him, and the patients who acquiesce to his demands. It is
very difficult for such a man to come home to what he sees
as confusion and neglect. And for what? Just so his wife
can piddle around in work that he regards as trivial compared to his profession. And therein lies another major
difficulty for a doctor's wife who attempts reentry. For a
woman who has never worked before, or at least not for
many years, the prospect of seeking a job is fraught with
fears and crippling insecurities. She sees herself as un-
qualified, with no experience, references, or marketable
abilities. She has no understanding of how to apply for jobs,
how to project herself at interviews, how to handle herself
in the busines world. She needs a heavy dose of support to
shore up her battered psyche, and her husband is the logical
source. But if he is a doctor with the attendant ego and
overblown sense of his own importance, he will at best
condescend to her little efforts, or at worst, denigrate them
for fear of the potential risk to his comforts. He may not
state his opposition overtly, but may keep up a flow of
subtle, demoralizing digs or undermine her morale thoroughly by refusing to take her entire plan seriously. One
doctor of my acquaintance did pretend to encourage his

wife in her attempts to go back into her premarriage career because he never really believed anyone would consider her valuable enough to hire. However, when she triumphantly announced she had found a job, to start on Monday, he announced he was suddenly exhausted and she must make immediate arrangements for a trip for them to Jamaica. A major confrontation ensued, and the result was that he went to Jamaica alone.

Assuming the doctor's wife does not allow all these obstacles to deter her and ultimately finds a job, new pitfalls await. Since she has not worked for many years, or is starting in a field that is totally new, her lack of recent experience will presumably put her into a lower echelon position. Remember, this is a woman who is accustomed to sitting atop the status ladder as "the doctor's wife." This sudden relegation to a subordinate posture as befitting her capabilities and not her husband's is a bitter pill. After being persona very grata everywhere, sought after socially, invited to assume positions of authority and respect in the community, she may find it hard to accept this instant demotion. And then if she does handle the come-down, she is faced with resentment from her co-workers. "Why the hell are you taking a job? [inference: away from someone else] You certainly don't need the money!"

She's damned if she asserts her independence by going to work, and damned if she doesn't and chooses to stay home to reap the rewards of maritally acquired cash and cachet.

When she does find a job that she enjoys and excels in, or if she has a career or profession that she practices with pride, there's another major frustration coming her way. Doctors' wives are prone to be victimized by the comments of insensitive people who regard any work performed by the spouse of a doctor as of minimal importance compared to the fascinating life-saving achievements of her husband. What could she possibly do that is more dramatic, more exciting, more admirable, than curing people and saving lives? Here is a "Guest Corner" column submitted to *Medical/Mrs.* by Liz Hancock, who is a highly skilled pediatric registered nurse at a California hospital. It conveys the resentments of the professional wife of a physician whose truly important work is constantly diminished by evaluative comparison comments and attitudes that pit her job against her husband's.

Why Should His Career Overshadow Mine?

When asked that tiresome and bothering question so prevalent at social gatherings, "And what do you do, Mrs. Doctor?" the gnawing innuendo implied haunts me and others like myself. Perhaps because the unspoken question remains, "Could what you do possibly be more interesting and intellectually rewarding than your husband's profession?"

Immediately I feel my defenses tightening, and try as I might to reply confidently as to what I do, I wind up feeling upstaged. For no matter what I do, and this applies not only to doctors' wives but all women married to professionals, the fact that my husband is a physician will seem a more stimulating source of conversation. The queries directed at him regarding his career and opinions spark an irrational seed of jealousy within me, though he can hardly be held accountable. From deep within a familiar voice screams, "Hey? What about the fantastic job I have?" even though it hasn't managed to reach the surface yet.

For example, my husband and I recently attended a social event where uncharacteristically he was the only M.D. there. When the inevitable question arose, I replied matter of factly, "I'm a pediatric registered nurse at the local hospital." Mind you, whether a nurse, housewife, etc., the scenario does not change. The replies were forthcoming and as usual predictable. "How nice. I'll bet it's interesting being married to a doctor. By the way, just what type of doctor is your husband?" My consternation over this subordination of my profession has not mellowed over the years. Instead the indignation has increased and I find myself becoming incensed at the lack of opportunity to explain what I consider my multifaceted and intellectually challenging job. Quite simply, no one really cares what I do, or even worse, they assume incorrectly that they already know. After all, just as "doctor's wife" evokes images of tanned tennis players and golfers, the registered nurse has its inherent misconceptions as well. From purveyors of bed pans to the doctor's right hand, nurses too have failed to project a precise image of what they actually do. Thus my problem becomes twofold. Not only am I considered an extension of my husband, but also an instrument to implement the phantom upper right extremity missing from those who wish to practice medicine.

"Damn it!," I want to shout. "Yesterday I recognized a potentially fatal arrythmia on one of my patient's electrocardiographic monitors and notified the M.D. in time. If it weren't for my professional expertise the child might have died. Now doesn't that interest you?" Instead they sit, oblivious to the fascinating facets of my career, hanging on every word my husband utters, because he is the *Doctor!* And though criticism of his profession abounds these days, he is still close to a deity outside medical circles.

For example, one member of these social gatherings can almost always be expected to ask for free medical advice in some disguised form. The fact that the questions are always directed at the doctor, though countless M.D.'s have wives who are nurses, is no surprise. After all, he is considered the expert, and most times rightly so. However, when the mother of a three-month-old infant inquires whether her son's sticky stools are the result of the addition of prunes to his diet, I feel almost compelled to reply, "How the hell would he know, he hasn't treated a kid for ten years!" Since my husband happens to be an internist, I'm often tempted to add, "However, if your stools are sticky, perhaps he can help."

Granted these types of interactions are not only unique

to doctors' wives. It seems almost inbred that many women fear upstaging their husbands' careers. I have watched with interest a well-known female neurosurgeon fade into the woodwork when her economist husband enters into animated conversation at the dinner table about the current financial ills of our country. Surely she must have something to say equally as absorbing if not more so.

I am also reminded of one of our local endocrinologists and his lawyer wife. Although she put her husband through medical school while working at a top-flight New York law firm, she rarely mentions her past career now that she is a retired mother of two. If conversation meanders toward her past accomplishments in the field of law, her husband not so subtly steers the focus away from her by introducing a topic related to his field. In other words, "That's right, folks, but let me tell you about the pituitary dwarf I saw for hypertension yesterday." And the fact remains that most people would rather hear about his strange medical anomaly. The mystique surrounding medicine continues to bathe the practitioner's ego in the limelight. Often this spotlight is not large enough to acommodate his wife.

Which leads me to my final point. The feedback that doctors receive about their chosen career usually serves to strengthen their sense of accomplishment. If they possess any doubts about their limited backgrounds in the art of common sense or broader education it is usually forgotten when asked the ever present question, "And what do you do?" The erroneous assumption by most that because he is a doctor he knows it all, is very reassuring to the shakiest of egos. Thus he often, like his wife, complacently accepts the stereotypes heaped upon him while he quietly nurtures a fear that it will be discovered he knows nothing at all outside of medicine.

And for the medical wife who may be suffering from a sense of lost accomplishments, riding on her husband's coattails may seem preferable to feeling like a nonentity. Surely there are many medical wives, or wives of professionals, who may have more exacting and challenging jobs than their husbands. But they are lost in the clamor at-

tended to their husbands' professions. Now that it is rea-
sonably fashionable for women to have careers outside the
home, the trend is slowly changing. Perhaps medical wives
in particular can hasten this process by asserting they are
capable of more than chauffering offspring or volleying on
the courts. This does not mean they must risk demeaning
their husbands in the process. Instead, by working together, each can reap the benefits of a more healthy and
accurate image. The time for change has never been riper.

There are many famous achievers in the ranks of doctors'
wives, such as Rita Moreno, Barbara Tuchman, the Pulit-
zer Prize winning historian, and Lenore Hershey, editor-in-
chief of *Ladies' Home Journal*. Even these women mention
the second-spot importance their jobs take in relation to
their husband's, a startling fact that emerged when I interviewed Lenore Hershey. I met her through a doctor friend
who had been seated next to her at a medical dinner and
mentioned the encounter casually. "I met another lady in
publishing last night," he said. "She mentioned that she had
just come from a visit with Claire Boothe Luce, but I
figured she's a crock." "What's her name?" I asked. "Hershey. She's Sol Hershey's wife." "You don't mean Lenore
Hershey?!" I asked in awe. "Yeah, that's the broad. I asked
her what she did and she said she was in publishing."

Now for Lenore Hershey to just say she's in publishing
is like Thomas Hoving, president of Tiffany's, to say he's
a shopkeeper. Lenore is a major name in publishing and
has been for over twenty years. But at a medical dinner, she
was just Sol Hershey's wife, not only in the eyes of the
doctors there, who regard all careers other than medicine
as trifling, but apparently in her own view as well. Here is
the interview.

"Men forge ahead for power . . . women long to achieve,"
said Lenore Hershey as we sat at her regular table in New
York's posh Four Seasons restaurant.

Lenore Hershey is a famous woman who has achieved success in both a man's and woman's world. As the editor-in-chief of *Ladies' Home Journal* and a vice-president of Downe Publishing Inc., she is listed in the *World Almanac* as one of the twenty-five Most Influential Women in America.

Lenore has been successful in another important area, too. She has been happily married for thirty-four years to Dr. Solomon G. Hershey, an anesthesiologist, and is the mother of a daughter, Jane, who is a free-lance writer.

"My career just seemed to develop," she mused. We were lunching at the famous "in" spot for the movers and shakers of the publishing world. When I arrived and mentioned the name "Lenore Hershey," I was instantly whisked to what was obviously a prime position in this famed establishment where the location of your table is an instant barometer of your status. Diametrically opposite sat Clay Felker, the recently deposed imperator of *New York* magazine and now publisher of *Esquire*. A steady stream of people stopped at our table—heads of corporations, names you read in the business pages every day; all had special greetings for Lenore.

This is the milieu in which Lenore Hershey moves comfortably. As head of the magazine that reaches fourteen million women monthly, she is a power in the nation, a guest in the White House, and one of the nicest, most down-to-earth women you'll ever meet.

How did she achieve this enviable position? Although she made it sound simple and natural, I know that work, drive and talent, plus the rare ability to take risks at the right time, are what made it all happen.

After she was graduated from Hunter College, where she majored in journalism, Lenore went to work in the publishing field. But in those days, women didn't rise on merit automatically; the lucky one found a male mentor who took her to the top with him.

"Yes, I had male mentors," she told me. "Like most men of the time, and today, too, they underestimated the capability of women." The comfortable idea was that a

woman presented no threat. She was at *McCall's* for fifteen
years, and then, in 1968, moved on to *Ladies' Home Journal* as subordinate to one of her mentors. She served as
managing editor and executive editor. Five years ago, when
her mentor left his position as editor-in-chief at the *Journal*, an opportunity presented itself and Lenore decided
to take the risk. "I asked the board to give me his job, that
I was sure I could do it. They decided to take a chance on
me." Her old boss was sure she'd fall on her face. Instead,
she led the magazine into a resounding lead position in the
industry and is today considered one of the foremost
editors-in-chief in the country.

As we lingered over coffee, I brought up the subject that
always interests me: How did she balance the roles of wife,
mother and career woman?

"There's never been any problem," she said with a smile.
"My husband has always been extremely supportive.
Surely, there were times Jane resented my work, but all
children dislike anything that takes mother away from
home, whether it be volunteer work or social engagements.
The fact is, today my daughter and husband feel our lives
were more interesting because of the facets my work
added."

As our enjoyable lunch came to an end with the ultimate
cachet of total absence of check ("I don't get one. They
just put it on my bill") ... I asked the last question. "How
does your husband feel about your national eminence?"

She laughed. "But there's never been any contest. I
always felt that Sol's profession involves life and death.
And no matter what so-called prominence I achieve, it can
never be more important in the scheme of things than his
work. When we go to medical conventions, I am Dr. Hershey's wife. When he comes to my meetings, he's Lenore
Hershey's husband. We're both proud of each other!"

Now, if an outstanding achiever in the vital area of com-
munications—a woman who can influence the opinion and
affect the emotions of five million women a month—
if such a powerful woman considers her work less important

than her husband's, what chance does the ordinary doctor's wife have for developing self-esteem? The facts are that whereas other professions or careers may deal in affecting the quality of life, the doctor deals directly with life and death—and that's a tough act to follow.

What Happened to the Queen-of-the-Community Image? The New Hostility to Medicine

"When you join an organization and people meet each other, they ask what your husband does. When you say 'doctor' it gets around the room and you sense the difference."

"No one ever had to ask me what my husband did. I mean the banners were out even before I came. I hardly walked through the door of our new condominium when the phone was ringing inviting me to something."

"Some people have cultivated our friendship just because we are a 'doctor and his wife.' Why should people invite Harry and me before even meeting us? I got the impression with some people that it was a social status thing. I don't think they'd have invited the new plumber in town the same way."

These were the comments made by a group of doctors'

wives to the question "Did you feel when you married a doctor that it would bring you a special respect from the community that perhaps other wives don't get?" Of course they expected instant status when they married doctors. It comes with the territory and was one of the positive factors influencing their decisions to marry. In the "Myth vs. Reality" survey for *Medical/Mrs.*, to the question "Did the image of a doctor's wife convey prestige to you?" 54 percent said "Yes." Since we do not have an aristocracy in this country, we tend to invent our own class system, and Mrs. Doctor becomes a queen by marriage.

Today, kings and queens and gods and goddesses are no longer spared from public potshots and critical review. The old respect for doctors is now tinged with resentment as they are being accused of avarice and their quest for cures is suspected of being overshadowed by their drive for dollars. As medical costs skyrocket, the daily newspapers carry stories about Medicaid mills that conspire with doctors to extort huge sums of money from the government for unnecessary medications, about physicians who overtreat elderly patients and send astronomically inflated bills to Medicare, and about medical misjudgments that impose horrendous tragedies upon patients who collect huge malpractice awards. The public still looks upon doctors as healers, but their noble motives are being impugned. After years of being regarded as revered wise men whose pronouncements were accepted without question, doctors are now subject to the same scrutiny and suspicion as executives, professionals, and businessmen. Doctors' wives are suffering from this new iconoclasm and are facing hostility they never anticipated when they signed on. "It's all Ralph Nader's fault," lamented one doctor's wife. As she sees it, consumer advocacy has created a questioning attitude toward all services, and the medical profession is an innocent victim.

"A large number of physicians sincerely believe that the

house of medicine is a fortress under siege, surrounded by hostile patients, aggressive unions, dictatorial government agencies, and domineering insurance companies. Their sense of being 'intruded upon' and 'interfered with' by laymen and their instrumentalities is implicit in many a private practitioner's perceptions of himself and the world around him." In an attempt to explain medicine's conservatism a psychiatrist member of the AMA Council on Mental Health said of the profession: "Paranoia is rampant, insecurity is rife."

Dr. James A. Halstead of Detroit, Michigan, states in the *New England Journal of Medicine*: "The diminishing prestige of the medical profession in the public eye is a matter that must concern the practicing physicians, medical educators and administrators as well as the leaders of organized medicine. . . . Dr. John S. Detar, former president of the American Academy of General Practice, speaks of 'untarnishing' the medical image."

Doctors are keenly aware of their deteriorating standing and there is much discussion on the topic in the medical community. Dr. Lindsay E. Beaton, former president of the Arizona State Medical Association, spoke of the eroding position of the doctor: "No demonstration is needed to prove that the physician has found himself in a chillier climate of national opinion in recent years. Traditionally, he was not only respected for his professional skills but beloved for his personal relationships with those for whom he cared. He was the accepted symbol of selfless devotion to duty. Today, he has undergone what often seems to him like systematic and studied deprecation. Beneath the rapturous platitudes about medicine with which we regularly beguile ourselves, let us note a hard fact: Many people now think of us as men concerned first with personal gain and only secondly with the welfare of the sick."

Strangely enough, while medical men are becoming manic about their tarnished image, a survey by the University of

Chicago's National Opinion Research Center indicates that the public ranks doctors second highest in occupational prestige, coming right after the Supreme Court.

Obviously the profession rates high, but the practitioners do not. The declining prestige of the physician has been caused by the new public skepticism of idols. And, as happened when the little boy proclaimed the emperor's nakedness, the physician is suddenly being exposed without his enchanted white coat, and what he presents is "a man of mediocre intellect, limited interests, trade school mentality and incomplete personality—the contemporary Non-Renaissance Man."

The public now sees the doctor as a man who is passionately devoted not to health care but to the disposal of his huge disposable income—which they, the public, have contributed to heavily. Expensive cars (currently Mercedes and Porsches lead), airplanes (there is a Flying Physicians Association), and lavishly appointed boats (one of the nation's largest yacht sales firms reports that doctors and dentists account for 25 percent of their power boat sales) are some of the toys that doctors collect. Remembering that most doctors have slaved away in virtual penury for many years during training, their ostentatious spending when they hit their $75,000 annual median income stride is understandable. Doctors are usually "new money," which is why purveyors of luxury products and services love their custom. "Doctors' wives come in here and want instant heirlooms," reports a large antique dealer. Real estate salespeople report that doctors and their wives seek conspicuously affluent homes. That physicians are avid vacationers and seekers of costly sybaritic pleasures is attested to by the existence of a magazine called *Diversion*, which is entirely devoted to leisure pursuits for physicians only. Country clubs, golf clubs, tennis clubs . . . doctors wallow in a display of the accoutrements of wealth that is hard to reconcile with the old romantic image of the dedicated scientific healer.

They offer up a social portrait of a shallow, nonintellectual conformist (a basic element in the medical personality) who spends his office hours in the pursuit of high fees and his leisure hours in the pursuit of self-indulgent high living. Not too sympathetic a figure, especially when viewed by a patient who has just received a $77,000 hospital bill (as did a relative of mine) plus charges of $60 from the podiatrist who came in to trim the patient's toenails, and $500 from the dermatologist who walked in twice to prescribe salve for a bed rash.

The extent to which this new community animosity has affected physicians' families is apparent from this article which was written by a doctor's wife for *Medical/Mrs.*

Facing the Fee Factor

"Thirty-five dollars. Can you imagine the nerve?" the out-raged woman cries. "That doctor charged me thirty-five dollars for a fifteen-minute visit. He expects me to pay for his new Mercedes."

How often has the doctor's wife found herself listening to such outbursts? "Countless times," says Patsy Lewis, wife of a urologist. "And not just myself. Even our children have been reduced to tears by schoolteachers who are openly hostile towards doctors."

There can be no doubt that a great deal of adverse publicity is currently directed towards the medical profession. Charges of too many overequipped hospitals in large cities, not enough physicians in rural areas, unnecessary laboratory tests, and, in quite the most frequent allegation, doctors, generally portrayed as lupine and avaricious, getting paid too much money for too little attention.

These accusations are made with increasing frequency in newspaper columns, editorials, magazine articles, car pools and supermarket checkout lines. Undoubtedly, there are doctors who charge whatever the traffic will bear, but they are a minority.

A dozen telephone calls to local doctors with various

specialties resulted in an average fee of $29.28 for an initial
visit, with subsequent visits running ten dollars less. Compare this figure to the $19.95 charged by Sears Roebuck
and the $15.95 by General Electric for a service call, and
the patient, it would seem, is getting a better deal than the
appliance owner in terms of value for services rendered.

How does the physician's wife react when she finds herself confronted by a neighbor, angered over what she considers to be excessive fees? Without exception, all those
interviewed admitted to being defensive. "I try not to be,"
says Patsy Lewis, "but I always am. I tell them I am not
going to make it my career to defend the medical profession or to apologize for the situation. I come from a family
of very successful businessmen and there is absolutely no
comparison between the income of a successful businessman and that of a doctor."

Because success in this country is measured in terms of
dollars, doctors often find themselves in a double bind. On
the one hand, if they live in an affluent neighborhood, it is
assumed that they must be overcharging their patients.
On the other, if they own a modest home in a less affluent
part of town, they are assumed to be incompetent.

Many doctors' wives are making a conscious effort not to
be defensive, but as the issue is loaded with emotional
overtones, this often proves difficult. Gloria Young, who
is married to an anesthesiologist, admits she occasionally
tries to explain. "But then," she says, "I get mad at myself.
Most people have no idea of how much free medicine our
husbands give. Actually, most people in the business community live a lot better than we do."

Few of the wives interviewed were able to handle such
confrontations objectively. One woman merely refers all
such complaints to the local and state medical societies.
"I give them the names and addresses of the chairmen of
the ethics committees," she said coolly, "and tell them if
their complaints are valid they will be dealt with effectively."

A surgeon's wife has evolved her own method. She
listens, then asks politely, "Does your grocer charge you for

food according to your ability to pay? Did your butcher ever give you free meat because you couldn't afford it? My husband devotes one day a week treating people in a clinic, totally free. In his private practice, he charges according to the patient's ability to pay. Does anyone else you deal with do that?"

Some of the complaints, of course, are not valid. The woman in our example feels that thirty-five dollars is too much money for a mere fifteen minutes of her doctor's time. She has no way of knowing how many hours he spends each week reading medical journals and studying new literature to keep abreast of developments in his field. Therefore, she cannot possibly consider the benefits she gains from this extra time invested by him.

Quite probably, as a doctor's wife, nothing you say will convince your angry neighbor that her physician's bill is not out of line. She studies your nice suburban home, reasons that your children go to private school, is aware of your membership in the local country club. How does she know so much about you, this woman who is justifying her complaints by judging your affluence? More than likely, she lives a few blocks from you, her children attend the same school as yours and she is a member of the same country club. In other words, her family income is equal to, if not higher than, yours.

The public does not look upon medical practice as a business incurring overhead such as office rental, nurses' salaries, malpractice insurance and expensive diagnostic equipment (taking, as it does, considerably more than a stethoscope to set up practice these days). Rather, they prefer the romantic notion of Drs. Schweitzer and Dooley, dedicating their lives to the good of man. Translated into terms of the seventies, however, the primitive leper becomes your average hypertensive executive and the romance loses something in the translation.

The fact that medicine is a service and services are intangible commodities has a great bearing on current feelings. It is a feature of our materialistic society to resent paying for something one cannot hold in one's hand. The good feeling alone, derived from wearing a new dress, is well worth the price of the article. But what does one do with a gall bladder?

If the architect's wife, the lawyer's wife, the business man's wife is not asked to justify the family income, why should the doctor's wife allow herself to be railroaded into defending an economic level that differs little from that of her critics?

Try though they may to avoid the uncomfortable position, doctors' wives are being driven into a defensive posture and they cannot always cope. Younger women are more accustomed to handling these challenges, but the older wives, who had been treated with honor and courtesy, are thrown by the new disrespect. They're puzzled, shocked, and angry. This article from a doctor's wife of nearly twenty years explains how she handles the problem.

Random Rules for Doctor-Wifing

Although medical families and other interested audiences are subjected frequently to a variety of learned discussions, particularly via the media, about the physician's badly battered image, there appears to be no such public interest in the image of the doctor's wife. Believe me, she does have one and I think that I would be performing a beneficent service to less seasoned medical wives were I, a 20-year veteran of doctor-wifing, to share a few of my own time-tested rules for surviving in that sometimes hazardous position.

Stock situations exist and can be anticipated. One of the more common, especially in suburban areas, is the dress shop confrontation with one of your husband's patients. (At the moment I am usually forcing my size 14 into a size 12 that I just know will be perfect for me after two weeks of dieting I am going to begin immediately.) You are both trying on dresses and she will inevitably spot you first, which gives her the advantage because she knows you and you have no idea of who she is. With a wistful smile she will greet you, "Hi, Mrs. Doctor. Buying a new dress? Or dresses, I suppose? Me? I'm just looking, really. We just paid your husband's bill and we'll be lucky if we can manage the groceries for the next two months. But enjoy your new wardrobe. We want someone to get our money's worth."

In my salad days, I would meet these remarks head on with an inane and furious answer. Something brilliant like, "Your husband doesn't make a salary, lady? You walk around naked, chum?" No more. The most I allow myself is what I believe to be a gracious smile, dazzling her with my expensive capping job, and a charming, "Thank you so much. I appreciate your generosity." This is guaranteed to stop her just long enough for you to squirm out of whatever garment you are in, toss it to the winds, and make for the nearest exit.

Always remember that you are married to a doctor and therefore, as everybody knows, your supply of cash is endless. Not for you the worry about mortgages, insurance premiums, and school tuition payments—all of which come due on the same day. To reinforce this illusion of eternal affluence, always turn unpaid house bills face down on your desk (or orange crate, if you're still paying back the inevitable medical school loan). Why look at them, since you probably won't be able to pay them for another two months? These are the same genre of bills that the patient receives, and he is very apt to slide by the doctor's bill "one more time" because "the doctor isn't pinched for money like real people are." In our family, one dependable income tax deduction is for late payment charges and loan interest.

If your teenagers want a job after school or during a vacation, they will be accused of depriving more needy youngsters of a job. If your husband hires them to work in his office, to answer the phone or clean up the filing that his staff never has the time to do, he will be accused of using them nepotistically to cheat the IRS. Since these are facts of medical family life, the only track you can follow is to put them to work in the cellar, the attic, or the backyard and pay them minimum wage out of your own pocket.

And then, like all other parents, love them a lot, pray hard, and they will turn out just fine.

With good luck, your children may follow in their father's footsteps and provide a second job for you— doctor-mothering—and that requires another whole new set of rules.

Nowhere does this new dethroning of doctors become more evident than in the proliferation of malpractice suits. The very word *malpractice* sends shock waves of anger and indignation through any group of doctors and their spouses. Consistent with a narcissistic belief in their infallibility, doctors have placed the blame for malpractice mayhem on lawyers, which is like attributing a killing to the gun instead of the murderer. The new view that medical men should be held accountable for their errors and misbehavior, as are all other mortals, is a concept that most doctors regard as heresy. The usual argument is that medical practitioners are reviewed by peer groups, who are the only people capable of judging the validity of procedures. However, a review of their reviews indicates a large reluctance on the part of physicians to chastise other physicians, and the number of doctors who had been deprived of the right to practice by their peers is minimal.

In New York in 1960 when the state government took action against 216 doctors, the medical societies saw fit to punish *none*. In 1963 in California, the state took 59 actions against physicians, the local medical societies, just *two*. In Oregon, the state acted against 56, the medical groups *four*. In Florida, the state 14 and the medical groups *zero*. The total state actions against doctors in that year totaled 401; there were only 82 medical society actions, and none at all in 30 states.

Now that the mammoth malpractice insurance premiums have made them painfully aware of the personal penalty for protecting each other from public censure, doctors are being forced to police their own numbers. But accepting blame comes very hard to doctors who have been accustomed to reverence and blind obedience. Their recourse has been to seek a scapegoat, and the legal profession has been elected as the one most doctors love to hate. There is a bumper sticker you will see on doctors' cars that reads: "Support lawyers— send your son to medical school." At one of our group meetings, a doctor's wife reported that her daughter had recently married a lawyer and her husband looks upon him as an enemy and has not permitted him to enter their home. My own gynecologist immediately became my ex-gynecologist when he refused to examine my thyroid because "the area above the neck isn't covered by my malpractice insurance." He went on to explain how my bereaved family could sue him if I died of a thyroid malady and then launched into a tirade about the avarice, chicanery, and larceny basic to all lawyers, which he topped off with this ringing conclusion: "All lawyers are immoral and devious and just a quirk of fate has made them lawyers instead of criminals."

A young orthopedic surgical resident explained the new malpractice-affected procedures in the emergency room of his hospital in chilling detail. "When a seriously injured child comes in, we notify the administration office to reach the parents for approval of surgery. In the old days we would've just operated immediately. Now we tell them upstairs to hurry because the kid has only a half hour. If they can't reach the family within that time, we get a call from the office telling us to get the hell out of there and not to be near when the kid dies so that we can't be sued for malpractice."

Doctors and their wives see the whole matter of malpractice suits and new assertion of patients' rights as a conspiracy against their profession by unscrupulous ignoramuses. They had become so conditioned to the pedestal position that they cannot cope with the antagonism and assaults from the disenchanted public, whose conditioning has gone through a metamorphosis that results in questioning all authority. The situation has driven doctors and their wives into a state of mass paranoia illustrated by an article we received (and returned) from a doctor's wife in which she outlined the hypothesis that the malpractice lawsuit is the newest concept in Yankee capitalistic enterprise. No investment, no overhead, all you need is a doctor to sue and a lawyer to handle the case and you get rich quick.

It does seem a rather simplistic rationale for a serious situation, but doctors and their wives view the current hostility to medicine in basic black-and-white terms and see the resultant damages to health care as being caused by the community attitude and not the doctors' actions.

Malpractice suits are having a deleterious effect on the practice of medicine and are driving up the costs of health care. True.

Doctors now subject patients to endless and costly tests, no matter how remote their relationship to the symptoms exhibited, in order to prevent accusations of misdiagnosis later on. True.

Doctors are forced to practice defensively and cannot act on instinctual gut reaction for fear of prosecution if the patient dies. True.

All true and all contributory to the astronomically escalating costs of health care. But what about the contributory negligence of the medical profession that brought on these extreme conditions? Doctors and their wives overlook the fact that for years the closed ranks of the medical profession chose to ignore the dangerous incompetence of many doctors, and rather than censure them or in any way deprive them of their elegant livelihoods, allowed them to continue mistreating and misdiagnosing patients.

The AMA itself, in the underpublicized Truman report, stated: "We conclude that the present supervision of organized medicine over the ethical standards of doctors is not adequate to protect the public, or the good name of the profession." The AMA's Medical Discipline Committee concurred: "All too seldom are licensed physicians called to task by boards, societies, or colleagues."

As for policing itself, this is a myth perpetuated by the medical profession. "I do not believe the AMA is sponsoring self-policing in the same way as the legal profession," Dr. Robert E. Shank, then AMA committee chairman, testified before a Senate subcommittee hearing. "I know in my state I have seen examples of gross medical negligence go uncensored, and the victim could not even get an award in court from the damages resulting from negligence."

The fact is, doctors always hid behind "medical ethics" as the excuse for avoiding discussion of a colleague's error with the laity. An AMA survey showed that 58 percent of physicians believed that most doctors tried to hide other doctors' mistakes. No matter how flagrant a doctor's error or behavior, it was almost impossible to find a fellow physician who would be willing to testify against him. They maintained a conspiracy of silence that offered protection to themselves but not the public. The medical profession is only now paying the price for those years of insular elitism; the once inviolate perfection of their world has been shattered by reality and it can never be the same again.

But one aspect of the community attitude toward doctors' wives has not changed. That is the widely held assumption that because she is related to the physician and lives with him, the doctor's wife can diagnose illness and prescribe cures. And it's so much better to ask her than him because it's free.

The spouse of a physician is constantly beleaguered by telephone callers who ask for her advice. "I have a little question that I know you can answer because I don't want to disturb the doctor." (Translation: "to get a bill.")

Here is how Marguerette Hosbach, a pediatrician's wife

from Norwich, New York, handles professional medical queries with aplomb and without risk.

Each day be at attention for the dinnertime telephone caller, usually female, who says, "Mrs. Doctor, I have a tiny little question that I know you can answer and I don't want to disturb Doctor because I know how important his time is." You, you must understand, are reading Gothic novels and chewing up chocolates as you lie on the chaise longue on your patio. No sense in telling the caller that you have a meal burning on the stove. She is never going to believe that you don't have a live-in cook. Just be as polite as your mother taught you to be and make sure that the fire extinguisher is within easy reaching distance.

An absolute of doctor-wifing is that you must be ready at all times to discuss illness—other people's. At the hairdressers, at the supermarket, out-of-doors in the rain while waiting for the kids to come out of school, going down the steps after church (an ideal place because a good crowd can gather), and especially at parties, where a strong stomach is a definite asset. Try popping a hot hors d'oeuvre into your mouth while the person next to you is graphically describing his youngster's gastroenteritis. If your husband is with you on any of these occasions, it is useless to attempt to reach him for cover. He will be fenced in on all sides by people amazing him with stories of their almost fatal illnesses and subsequent miraculous recovery.

To tell the truth, I have never really found a successful diversionary tactic for these situations, except perhaps the feigning of a light head and nausea. This combination of symptoms, mentioned by you in a small breathless voice while you are weaving gently back and forth, ensures that everyone near you will make a wide swath so that you may exit quickly for the nearest ladies' room.

You may be a physicist, attorney, executive secretary, or movie star, but make it easy on yourself and accept the dictum that you are a nurse. All doctors' wives are nurses, with or without a diploma. Over the past two decades I have not been able to convince one person that I am an

English teacher. I must be a nurse. Doctors only marry nurses. Watch any daytime soap opera for confirmation of that fact.

The natural sequela of this is that when Doctor isn't available, you will be able to tell the patient what to do. Now this is touchy territory—how to give comfort without inviting a malpractice suit. I have found that a lot of clucking sounds works wonders. These clucks should be accompanied by, "I know Doctor will want to talk to you just as soon as he comes in." This convinces the patient that his is a unique and extraordinary symptomology and that is why nurse-wife cannot prescribe.

The presumption that a doctor's wife knows more about illness than the layman is to a large extent justified. Given her years of identity with his profession, plus the fact that a large part of her social life revolves around doctors, which means she is exposed to a good deal of shop talk, she has absorbed some medical knowledge and is probably more familiar with drugs and diseases than are people who are not related to the health-care field. But what seekers of free advice from the doctor's distaff really expect is that when stumped, she will discuss the case with her husband and relay his advice—at no charge. What they don't know is that doctors hate to encounter sick people when they get home—and that means their families.

A major complaint from doctors' wives is that when they or their children get sick, the last person to turn to is their live-in physician. The old shoemaker's-children syndrome comes into play here as the doctor is either too emotionally drained from the day's labors to face illness in the home he has come to for respite or too emotionally involved to deal efficiently with a sick member of his own family.

"We've had a couple of medical crises where one of the kids went into shock," said a Connecticut doctor's wife. "Jerry had no Adrenalin at home when it happened and he knew what was going on and he just cried. They can't be objective. Every symptom in your own kid is magnified five hundred times."

The problem of medical care for the medical family was discussed by Drs. Lawrence and Myra Hatterer in a *Medical/Mrs.* column that answered my query: "When I or members of my family are ill, I often have the feeling that we are not getting the proper treatment. Am I overanxious?"

Dr. Lawrence J. Hatterer speaks:

The feeling you have, that of concern or anxiety in the face of illness, is a very common one for doctors' wives. It is important to identify which one it is.

The old adage that the "shoemaker's children go barefoot" often applies to the families of physicians. In that instance you would feel concern. It is not surprising that after working with sick people all day, the physician would like to return home to a pleasant, work-free environment. To assure this, he may unconsciously turn off illness as soon as he arrives home. He may not hear what you are saying or notice that you are ill. Unconscious mechanisms, such as leaving his bag in the car after you have asked him to bring it home, no prescription pads, all the thermometers being broken, are common.

Not only physical illnesses are ignored, but emotional ones, like depression and alcoholism, are dismissed as "menopausal" or "normal."

Often doctors treat their families as they do themselves. For various psychological factors, many operate with denial about their own illnesses. They rarely consult other doctors about themselves, deny their own mortality, and sometimes mistrust other doctors as a projection of their own insecurity. The early training which physicians have received that had enabled them to deal psychologically with illness objectively often breaks down when they themselves or their families are involved. Some doctors overreact to their family's illnesses. Because of their love, they may not be able to tolerate their family's suffering. Overreaction may bring overtreatment. Too much medication may be given, too much coddling prescribed. All of these would cause concern.

On the other hand, sometimes the feelings are those of anxiety. Deeper ones, caused by conflict within you. Doctors often rely on their wives to take over many of their responsibilities. Over the years, you may have been assigned to be "house physician." The conflict between being a good mother, good wife, good physician, and your own lack of knowledge, may be strong and anxiety-producing. Often a doctor's wife, because she has borne the major responsibility in the family, takes her role too seriously. This, combined with bits and pieces of medical knowledge gained from conversations at home, can cause her extreme anxiety.

As in all problem-solving, it is important first to identify the source of difficulty. Is it within yourself or in the attitude of your husband? Many doctors have avoided the conflict early in their marriage by engaging other physicians to take care of their children, their wives, and, in the most enlightened cases, themselves. By discussing with the attending physician the difficulties that can arise, they are minimized. Statements such as "please treat my family as you would any other patient" and "do not assume that we have any medical knowledge" helps the attending physician. In doing so, the wife can call her pediatrician, gynecologist, etc., as would any other wife.

Dr. Myra S. Hatterer speaks:

Sometimes you may feel like the "shoemaker's children" because it is not easy to get to your husband when it comes to the family's health needs. What's more, you may feel that he does not listen, or is not as alert to your emotional problems as he is to his patients'. What should you do?

You are really faced with the problem of how much your husband can give of himself after a long and often taxing day of giving to others. How often and in what way you approach him, along with his own innate capacity to give of himself, are among the important variables to take into account. Does he require inordinate recognition, concrete reward or adulation of his authority in order to give to you and the family? Is he only capable of giving to patients because of his total control over them, whereas in relation to his family, he feels blocked, or unable to exercise these controls? Do you fight him? Do your children rebel at his authority?

Still another variable to consider is his fear of treating his family. Does he feel that his own subjectivity, emotionality and guilt, should he maltreat or fail to help you, would be too painful for him to endure? His guideline might be "only a fool treats his own family." Find out! In some cases your husband's sheer exhaustion from overwork at the office/hospital/house calls/teaching/writing/research makes him shut off his mind and feelings to home work. To listen to a family member who becomes a patient (i.e., has a physical and/or emotional problem) is the last thing he can, wants to, or will do at the end of a demanding day. Everyone has had a piece of him. Now the family moves in for its piece, often with little or no awareness or caring about what he has been through that day. They only have a natural expectation that as husband/father/lover/companion/mentor, and doctor, too, his responsibility is to listen and to do something about their physical and emotional health. It is their human right.

After you have assessed these variables and taken as many of the above factors into account, asked yourself the appropriate questions, and are satisfied with reasonable anwers, then make a move. In some cases it should be right to phone for another doctor, recommended by your husband or by a reliable colleague. In others, a short, unpressured dialogue as to what would be best to do. Do this at a time when he is most relaxed and receptive to listening, not just as he reorbits from work into home. There are those unusual instances where his persistence and consistent neglect has provoked serious emotional and/or physical destructiveness to one or more member of the family. Your husband must be confronted with the seriousness of his withdrawal by having to face the consequences of his behavior. He and/or the family as a group may need and should seek out professional help to prevent any progressive deterioration of the situation. Denial by one or all persons involved is the most dangerous defense to such a life situation.

In the last analysis, you must be aware that even though your husband is a doctor, he has to be understood as a person who possesses all the same faults, limitations and potentials to disappoint and neglect you, as does any other human being. His career identity is one of service. However, he cannot and should not be expected to live that role around the clock. But don't be afraid to tell him, and ask him to live it with you and your family, to a reasonable degree.

Where the wife is overanxious, awareness of herself and her overall situation is important. When she has had to assume total responsibility, this should be addressed, not the issue of illness. Open discussion between herself and her husband is important. She may find that her husband was unaware of the burden she felt was placed on her shoulders, and, indeed, would in no way consciously want her to assume that responsibility.

Some doctors respond to family illness by downplaying the importance of the symptoms, others by distributing pills too freely. In all cases the primary inclination is to dispense fast solutions so that the unpleasantness will disappear from the home scene quickly. In her book, *How to Be a Doctor's Wife Without Really Dying,* Marguerite Hurrey Wolf says, "Our children learned at their father's knee that there is only one of two possible answers to the question 'What should I do about this, daddy?' Either 'Soak it' or 'Forget it.' . . . In defense of the doctor in the family, I must say that while knowing the patient helps in diagnosis, being related by paternity makes the doctor look at his child with blurred, double, or too sharply focused vision. He is not unaware of his family's health; he just prefers to assume it to be good." She concludes her chapter with, "If it is medical treatment for the family you want, you should have counted a few more buttons and stopped on lawyer or merchant. These men buy medical care the way we buy groceries or shoes for the children. Can you imagine living like that? Of course not, and better not try because it's not in your future. That's for OTHER people. You are different. You are a doctor's wife."

X

Would You Want Your Daughter to Marry One?

Doctors' wives tell the tale over and over again of marriages entered into with eagerness and the expectation of living a wonderful life with a wonderful man who will provide security and prestige, love and devotion.

Well, two achieved goals out of four isn't bad, but when the missing ingredients are vital to happiness and fulfillment, how important can the the remaining elements be?

Of the doctors' wives who responded to the *Medical/ Mrs.* survey, 54 percent said they would NOT encourage their daughters to marry doctors. Yet 77 percent stated they enjoyed being doctors' wives. Now if they like the role so much, why not wish it for their daughters, for whom mothers usually want only the best life has to offer?

Because they well know that their daughters will never make the compromises that they did . . . that the current generation is more concerned with the emotional quality of life that love and caring will provide rather than with the superficial pleasures that money and social position will provide, as this letter from a doctor's wife indicates: "It seems that if one is successful in marriage it's because one has cared enough to try very hard to make it work, and I have given in a lot and not made my wishes number one. I think perhaps my daughters are too 'liberated' to be like this in their marriages."

As a young doctor's daughter told me, "Never home, never there when you need him, always taking care of other people instead of you—what kind of husband is that? My mother puts up with that bullshit because she loves being Mrs. Doctor. But not me. I'll get my self-value from my own achievements. What good is all that money if you have no one to enjoy and share the goodies with?"

The New York woman who wrote saying, "Who cares about the marriage when you get to drive your Lincoln to the club every day?" may have been joking, or maybe not. But implicit in this black humor is a sad reality. The love/ hate attitude toward their marriages is a common thread that runs through the lives of doctors' wives. Theirs is the painful disillusionment of women who embarked on the marital relationship expecting familial fulfillment only to discover that their husbands are heroes in the workplace but failures at home. The full realization of the doctor's defects as a husband and father becomes apparent only gradually, according to the *Medical/Mrs.* survey, usually after the third year of marriage, because one prefers not to recognize such a major disappointment. Then the unhappy wife starts evolving ways to improve the relationship; after all, every marriage goes over rocky terrain, and adjustments must be made along the way. So she tries talking it out when she catches him, and maybe he vows to change, as she devises ways to improve their togetherness. More time goes by and nothing changes. By the time she accepts the fact that this man she married is a narcissistic, implacable, even remote individual who will always be a doctor first and a husband and father second, the arrangement has been carved in stone. By now, she has been seduced by the tangible benefits of

being Mrs. Doctor and is loath to give up the perks that
come with the job. And that's when the process of justifica-
tion, rationalization, and denial goes to work to enable her
to accommodate to this demeaning derivative life and accept a marriage that will never offer the kind of truly shared
relationship from which she can draw emotional sustenance.

"Have you been forced to make many emotional compromises in your marriage?" Sixty-four percent of the doctors' wives who responded said "Yes."

"Do you believe your husband has made any for you?"
Fifty-four percent said "No."

Many wives do a fantastic job of accepting the secondary
status of their needs in a medical marriage and work out
successful compromise lives for themselves that are con-
tingent but not dependent upon their husbands. Here are
letters from some such women:

> In medicine, the doctor has a consuming passion. For the
> spouse to sit at home pleading for more time is to enter
> the relationship from a position of weakness. You become
> part of the chorus demanding attention. Playing "poor
> me" rarely solves anything.
>
> For me, the solution has been in having my own inter-
> ests, balancing them with mutual interests. When I'm
> away from my husband, I'm doing things which com-
> pletely occupy me, bringing interesting things back to our
> time together. We have to add something besides de-
> mands to the marriage. The times when I have tried to live
> vicariously through my husband have been a disaster. Sec-
> ondly, we need a common interest different enough from
> medicine to be a welcome relief. For us, this includes heavy
> religious commitment, travel with and without our chil-
> dren, hiking new roads, swamps, woods. For others, it
> could be a sport, music, drama, or whatever. When both
> members of the couple look forward to that time off to-
> gether to see that new play, explore that strange cliff,
> pound that last nail . . . a lot of strain disappears.
>
> To sit at home moaning about the problems of being a

doctor's wife will only intensify the problems. Creative solutions do a better job.

Another doctor's wife puts it this way:

> I would say a doctor's wife must be self-sufficient. I taught school for thirty-two years. Since I was busy and raising two children, I didn't feel neglected by a very busy husband. I feel I contributed to his worthwhile life.

Still another wife explains her method of dealing with her marriage:

> A wife of any man must have a life of her own, too. There is sharing and companionship. But in a "service" marriage, when a spouse is service-oriented, the other spouse must be strong and carry the ball for family relationships.

Then there are those blissfully happy wives who plunge into the perks and pleasures of doctor wifehood and openly revel in the passalong prestige. (I even saw a Florida Cadillac with the license plate MRS. DR.) They have handled the unanticipated absence of intimacy and companionship by relegating these vital aspects of a real marital relationship to the classification of unimportant compared to the myriad benefits derived from being married to a doctor. This article from the newsletter of a New England medical society auxiliary demonstrates too well the satisfactions such women receive from this totally derivative identification.

Will the Real Doctor's Wife Please Stand Up?

> We all know well enough that the public's image of the doctor's wife is not what it should be. "They" gossip about us, write soupy, sick soap operas and portray us in television specials as whiny, rich nooses around the poor doctors' necks. And those movies (always rated R) are something to behold. The novels about doctors and their wives are

too hot to carry home from the book store. We're always gorgeous, slim, man-chasing, cocktail-drinking, bikini-clad pool sitters. We drive our Lincoln Continentals to the club for tennis after a daily appointment at our hairdresser's.

We should be so lucky! True. True. We are gorgeous. Some of us look good in a bikini. We have nice cars and like to relax around the pool with a cocktail sometimes. What the public doesn't or doesn't want to see is the real doctor's wife, the gal who volunteers her time in the community, at the bloodmobile, in the hospitals, in the schools, on the boards of volunteer agencies. You name it, if it's volunteer work, there's a doctor's wife who is involved. If we were to list (and we might just do that this year) all the volunteer work we do in the community, it would fill every page in that R-rated novel.

The unfortunate part of that involvement is that we are spread so very thin.

We have the luxury of being associated by marriage with the profession that still ranks number one in confidence and respect. Our husbands worked hard to achieve and retain that image and we, as physicians' wives, have a responsibility to help them maintain their good image.

We can do this by joining together and becoming involved in the community activities of the county auxiliary. We might not only improve our image and help our husbands maintain theirs but assist in improving the health and well-being of our people and succeed in making this a better place for ourselves, our families and for future generations.

These doctors' wives have learned to subordinate their needs to those of their husbands' and have evolved a seemingly satisfactory life structure based on their relationship to men of medicine. But not all women can feel whole in this secondary role. The price such self-denial exacts from the wife is pathetically expressed in this letter *Medical/Mrs.* received from a New England doctor's wife:

What's the matter with us doctors' wives? We have prestige, money and yet we are lonely a lot of the time. The
answer, of course, is to keep busy and we do—fund raising,
school board, church work—but I think a lot of doctors'
wives, if they are completely honest, feel there is a dimen-
sion of their lives that is absent.

The erosion of self-esteem in a person who knows that she
alone has made all the compromises is corrosive and constant. One of the major reasons that men make wars is to
satisfy their need to test themselves. After all, how many
of us encounter situations in daily life that reveal the basic
truth about ourselves, our abilities to react with strength
and honor when demanded? Facing up to one's weakness is
the most painful of human experiences. And that is exactly
what a doctor's wife who has allowed her individuality and
needs to be totally subordinated to those of her doctor husband must do every day. It is doubly devastating if she is
aware that she has made this soul-crushing compromise for
the sake of superficial satisfactions such as money, security,
and prestige. Ultimately the effort must take a terrible toll
on her ego and she will spend her life with a pervasive sense
of deprivation and sadness.

In her book *Behind Every Successful Man: Wives of
Medicine and Academe*, Martha R. Foulkes discusses the
painful choice doctors' wives have had to make.

But what of the needs of the wives themselves? How well
have their own expectations been met in their roles and
what has been the effect of being a wife on their own
growth and development?

For those women, most especially doctors' wives, who
have chosen to be in conventionally sex-typed, male-domi-
nated marriages, there has frequently turned out to be a
painful irony in their choice. The sort of man whom the
very traditionally defined female is most emotionally pre-
disposed to marry is, it seems, often the sort of man who is
most likely to let her down in the very relationship in

which she seeks her greatest satisfaction and rewards. The woman who marries with the idea of giving HER all to a man is usually inclined to marry a dominant, authoritative male who is usually inclined to give HIS all to a highly instrumental professional role, who is far better at receiving than returning devotion.

The hardest part of being a doctor's wife [says one of the forty women Ms. Foulkes interviewed] is sharing him. No, I would not want my daughter to marry a doctor. Most wives have problems with husbands as far as feeling that their husbands don't pay enough attention to them as to whatever business they're in. They double or quadruple that for a doctor. If you had asked me some years ago or even now on a bad day what I would change about his work, I would have some suggestions. I've gotten into his routines and I make my life around his. It's an alone life. I have let him know of my resentment of his practice. I resent it that I am not the only naked woman he has seen. It's another bit of sand on the pile of resentment. It's another thing I have to share that most wives don't.

Now this book is not meant to prove that *all* doctors' wives suffer from a paucity of companionship in their marriages and that *all* doctors are utter failures as husbands. A good deal of the quality of the doctor's input into his marriage has to do with his specialty as well as character, and there is a relationship between the two.

Dermatologists, anesthesiologists, radiologists, pathologists, ophthalmologists, and academic physicians lead programmed, orderly lives. Their hours are predictable, their time is scheduled, and they rarely have emergency calls. Terminal acne is an impossibility, and as an ophthalmologist told his near-hysterical young wife when she reached him on the golf course with an urgent message from the emergency room, "Honey, don't ever panic. No one dies from an eye problem." Besides the pleasant regularity of their lives, they do not suffer from the strain of having a minute-to-minute critical effect on the mortality of their patients. And since they do not constantly deal directly with life and death, they rarely develop the arrogant pomposity of the God complex.

When I interviewed the wife of an ophthalmologist, I entered the home with a large blank notebook and tapes, fully anticipating to exit hours later with a full complement of data on her methods of reconciliation with the problems of living with a physician and raising four children with an always absent father. I never even opened my notebook or switched on the tape recorder. The picture she painted was of a perfectly normal home life with a nine-to-six father who always had dinner with the family and maybe took off for an evening hour or two to make hospital rounds. He was a devoted father who arranged his hours and scheduled his operations to accommodate to his family's needs, never missed a graduation, school play, or Little League game. The facts as supplied by this doctor's wife seemed so unreal contrasted with the plaints I had come to expect from physicians' wives that I began to suspect I was facing a case of convincing self-delusion and denial. Then the children came home from school and I spotted the son in workshirt and jeans with long hair and beard. "Aha, the garb of the rebel," I thought. "Now I'll get the straight facts." But when he began to tell me about his swell "dad," I closed up my blank notebook and tape recorder and departed.

The same story was repeated with families of anesthesiologists, dermatologists, and the other specialties, where there was no indication that the doctor's profession in any way adversely affected the home or marriage. The assumption can be made that these areas of medicine attract men who prize family life and have made the decision that marriage and home come first and profession second, as with most normal nonworkaholic men. This conclusion is supported by these comments which came in on *Medical/Mrs.*

survey forms from wives of doctors in these less emotionally demanding specialties.

> My husband is a full-time staff specialist in a large hospital. As such, his hours are more regular and his schedule perhaps more flexible than private practitioners. This career choice was a deliberate choice due to his high priority placed on time with family.

> After my husband left a very busy family practice and specialized in anesthesia our life together and with our three children was much more ideal. We knew when he'd be on call and could work around those times.

> My husband is in emergency medicine, which is a new specialty. It allows him freedom at home from patients, nurses, and phone orders. He appreciates his time at home and I appreciate that.

> My husband is a radiologist, which is one of the less demanding specialties in terms of hours.

> My husband is an ophthalmologist, therefore our family life is maximal. His daily schedule is very predictable, much more so than neighbor executive friends. We do things together or not at all, i.e., skiing, sailing.

> My husband is a radiologist so the demands on his time outside of working hours are minimal. Family routines are seldom interrupted.

Women married to doctors who chose to enter the specialties that do not make the intense demands on time and emotions as do all other areas of medicine have little problem in reconciling their premarital expectations with the reality; they signed on for love, security, companionship, and prosperity and they got it. But the pain of the hundreds of thousands of doctors' wives who married with those same hopes and dreams and afterward encountered only deprivation and disillusionment are best expressed in this one wife's step-by-step answer to the *Medical/Mrs.* questionnaire.

Before Marriage

Q. Did you have specific thoughts about marrying a doctor?

A. My specific thoughts concerned marrying the man I was in love with. He was not even in a medical program when we were married, he was finishing his senior year in college.

Q. Was it a positive picture?

A. It definitely was a positive picture as far as marriage went, in fact we were so idealistic we were considering missionary work.

Q. If positive, was this reinforced by the media? family?

A. I worked as an R.N. in several hospitals, and when he decided to apply to medical school and was accepted, my opinion was reinforced by observation of the doctors with whom I worked and the doctor and his wife in whose home I lived while attending college.

Q. Did the image of doctor's wife convey prestige? security? happiness? pride?

A. Happiness—because we were so much in love.
Security—for a good life and finances for educating the family we hoped to have.
Pride—in being a part of making the world a better and healthier place to live in.

Q. Did a doctor present a romantic heroic image to you?

A. My husband seemed very romantic to me but his being a doctor did not affect me that way. I knew the hard work, lonely hours that were in store for us and I accepted it feeling our love, religious and family backgrounds, and trust in each other, our goals for the future would stand us in good stead.

Q. Did the fact that your future husband was to be a doctor affect your attitude toward him favorably?

A. Yes, it is an honorable profession, whether the man has honor is an entirely personal matter.

Q. Did you envision yourself as a helpmeet to a man of service?

A. Yes, I definitely did feel I would be his helpmeet, that my contribution toward his education, toward a happy well-cared-for home and family, a loving and understanding personal life would ease his way and his work would reflect that.

Q. Honestly, did you feel you had made a "good marriage" —achieved the everywoman's dream—when you married a doctor?

A. I felt I had married a good man because of our mutual beliefs and background, but I felt he had married a good woman, too. I understood his goals and knew they were good but I was not a "hero-worshipper" as far as his profession went. I felt and still do a man's or woman's profession should come fourth in the realm of priorities, God, Husband or Wife, Children and Family, then Work. Our problem I guess is that he doesn't nor ever has felt that way.

After Marriage

Q. How many years have you been married?

A. We have been "married" twenty-two years.
We were married thirty-one years ago.

Q. Did you help put him through medical school?

A. Yes, I worked while he went through medical school, internship and residency. His father and the government paid the bulk of the costs, my income went for rent and food.

Q. Have you been disappointed in any of your expectations?

A. Sorely so.

Q. If "yes," in approximately what year of your marriage did you become aware of your feelings?

A. In looking back I must have been aware of the changes in my husband and his antifamily behavior and rational-

ized by finding excuses and reasons why he had become
a different person—overwork, problems with the drug
scene in our children, school dropouts, and a teenage
pregnancy. But I wasn't aware of the real reason until
our twenty-sixth year of marriage.

Q. Do you feel deprived of companionship in your marriage?

A. Yes, though there are plenty of people about within the
family circle, neighbors, church, and socially, but the
lovely feeling of "oneness" is gone. I do not automatically think of us as a couple now. I attack a problem and
make decisions as a person now, perhaps that is good,
but I miss the sharing so in daily living.

Q. Do you resent your husband's absences and work demands?

A. I know how hard he works; I know he is a very good doctor up to a point. I resent his priorities in that I and the
children's activities seldom take first place in his considerations. He even felt he couldn't attend my mother's
funeral because of scheduled surgery and we had just returned from visiting my parents. My mother had spent
the entire week making sure we had a restful vacation.
I did resent very much his absences, but now I don't
care. I try to make sure he is aware of school and
church activities of the children and he often attends.

Q. Do you feel your husband's profession imposes an unfair
burden on you? On your children?

A. No, I do not feel his profession imposes an unfair
burden on me. I feel he does because he could control
and organize his time better if he really wanted to. There
again the children have had to live with his seldom attending their functions. If there is some effort made on
his part they are the first to recognize and appreciate his
presence, they yearn for it so. He is such a well-respected
figure in the community and he has helped so many
people, they can't help but want to share in the aura.

Q. Have you been forced to make many emotional compromises in your marriage?

A. Yes.

Q. Do you believe your husband has made any for you?

A. No or seldom. He never asks if his schedule conflicts with
   mine or the family's. We have to arrange ours around his
   if we want him present.

Q. Do you suffer due to the "God" status your husband
   enjoys?

A. I suppose so but in a different way than the question
   implies. Perhaps if I had shared that "God" status feeling he wouldn't have succumbed to that trap. I just felt
   he was a wonderful, wonderful man. The "God" status
   is reinforced constantly in his work, by coworkers and in
   the community. It's strange that the people who love
   him the most know how little he deserves it and still
   love him, yet he caters to this superficial adulation of
   community, hospital, and office staff.

Q. Did you realistically anticipate the difficulties in being
   a doctor's wife?

A. Evidently not. Being a doctor's wife is hard, being anyone's wife is demanding, being his wife was rewarding,
   but does one ever realistically prepare oneself for the
   humiliation and mockery connected with infidelity?

Q. Were your "before marriage" expectations met?

A. Yes, for twenty some years.

Q. Do you enjoy being a doctor's wife?

A. I do enjoy the aura of medicine, it is my profession too.
   I do enjoy the conversations I'm able to listen to and
   participate in and the friends I've made.
   I do enjoy the security of income for the educational
   demands we must meet.
   I do enjoy the trips to various parts of the country due
   to conventions. The joy of being my husband's wife is
   gone and he happens to be a doctor.

Q. If you had to do it again, would you marry a doctor?

A. I care so much more about the man's character than his profession, although I know your questionnaire implies profession contributes and dominates in so many ways. I also know any career or profession has its own particular kind of pressures and temptations. An adult man or woman makes their own choices.

Q. Would you encourage your daughter to marry one?

A. I would not encourage one of our daughters to marry a doctor but we already have a daughter who is married to a doctor. I can only pray they can maintain honesty, integrity, and honor toward each other and be one of the few doctor and wife marriages to prove a doctor can be a man of his word, or is that the impossible dream? One can have the right to all sorts of things by law or birth but unless these rights are honored by the people one lives with or among they don't do you one bit of good.

Notes

CHAPTER I

9   "What was surgery . . ." Lawrence Shainberg. *Brain Surgeon.* Philadelphia and New York: J. B. Lippincott Company, 1979, p. 94.

9–10   "The TV actor . . ." Joan Potter. "Soap Opera Surgeons." *Medical/Mrs.*, Vol. 1, No. 3, March/April 1978, pp. 24–5.

CHAPTER II

15   "In a study . . ." "Doctors and Divorce—Who's at Risk?" *Medical Opinion*, Vol. 2, June 1973, pp. 17–19.

16   "A lot of unmarried . . ." Reprinted by permission from pp. 49–50, 51, 56, Chapter 3, in *Making It in Medical School* by Robert H. Coombs and Joanne St. John. Coyright © 1979, Spectrum Publications, Inc., New York.

19   "For many entering freshman . . ." Ibid.

20   "When I came . . ." Ibid.

20   "I was top . . ." Ibid.

20   "PRE-MED STUDENT . . ." Ibid.

23   "A published profile . . ." "A Profile of the Medical Student." *CIBA Journal*, December 1, 1973.

25   "What causes those . . ." Myra Hatterer. *Medical/Mrs.*, Vol. 1, No. 4, June 1978, p. 35.

CHAPTER III

30   "The training left . . ." Shainberg. *Brain Surgeon*, p. 43.

33–34   "As 'fast-answer' . . ." S. Spence Meighan and Linda Osborne. "Adored at the Office—Abhorred at Home." *American Medical News*, Vol. 21, No. 37, September 22, 1978.

36   "it is a clinical . . ." James E. Miles, Robert Kress, and Tsung-Yi Lin. "The Doctor's Wife: Mental Illness and Marital Pattern." *International Journal of Psychiatry in Medicine*, Vol. 6, April 1975, pp. 481–2.

39–40   "Lament of the Wife . . ." Sonya Saroyan. *Nova Scotia Medical Bulletin*, December 1971, pp. 144–5.

46   "You get used to . . ." Shainberg. *Brain Surgeon*, pp. 29–30.

47   "A doctor gets . . ." Meighan and Osborne. "Adored at the Office . . ." *American Medical News*, September 22, 1978.

CHAPTER IV

54   "Betty's suspicion that . . ." Sally Schoiket. "The Physician's Marriage." *The Journal of the Medical Society of New Jersey*, Vol. 75, No. 2, February 1978.

54   "vehement aversion . . ." George E. Vaillant, Nancy Corbin Sobowale, and Charles McArthur. "Some Psychological Vulnerabilities of Physicians." Reprinted by permission from *The New England Journal of Medicine*, Vol. 287, August 1972, pp. 374–5.

54–55   "The role requires . . ." D. E. DeSole, P. Singer, and S. Aronson. "Suicide and Role Strain Among Physicians." *International Journal of Social Psychiatry*, Vol. 15, 1969, p. 294.

56   "A man's occupation . . ." Copyright © 1978 by Daniel J. Levinson. *The Seasons of a Man's Life*. New York: Alfred A. Knopf, Inc., p. 45.

56–57   "During early adulthood . . ." J. C. Donnelly. *"The Internship Experience: Coping and Ego Development in Young Physicians."* Doctoral Dissertation. Harvard University, 1979.

57 "At a stage . . ." Myra Hatterer. "Second Opinion." *Medical/ Mrs.*, Vol. 1, No. 3, March/April 1978, p. 17.

65–66 "There are many parallels . . ." Daniel H. Labby. "Don't Practice Assembly-Line Parenting." *Medical Economics*, October 1, 1979, p. 86.

69 "I never see him . . ." Arlene Garbett. "Dad's a Doctor, Big Deal!" *Medical/Mrs.*, Vol. 1, No. 3, March/April 1978, pp. 14–16.

69 "As much as his behavior . . ." Ibid.

72 "Patients put pressures . . ." Morton Glasser and Gretel H. Pelto. *The Medical Merry-Go-Round*. Pleasantville: Redgrave Publishing Company, 430 Manville Road, Pleasantville, N.Y. 10570, 1980, pp. 28–9.

CHAPTER V

81 "any stage of . . ." Joseph B. Trainer. "The Physician as a Marriage Counselor." *The Family Coordinator*, January 1973, p. 75. Copyright © 1973 by the National Council on Family Relations. Reprinted by permission.

82 "Many doctors-to-be . . ." Morton Hunt. "Where Sex Is Concerned the Doctor Is Out." *Playboy*, Vol. 26, No. 7, July 1978, pp. 134–6, 234–8. Originally appeared in *Playboy* magazine. Copyright © 1978 by Morton L. Hunt.

90–91 "Informants described fourteen . . ." James L. Evans. "Psychiatric Illness in the Physician's Wife." *The American Journal of Psychiatry*, Vol. 26, No. 7, pp. 134–6, 234–8, July 1978. Copyright © 1978, The American Psychiatric Association.

91–94 "Dr. Lawrence Hatterer replies . . ." Myra and Lawrence Hatterer. "Second Opinion." *Medical/Mrs.*, Vol. 1, No. 3, March/April 1978, p. 17.

95 "A young doctor . . ." Harold Marcus. "What Causes Those Medical School Marriages to Falter?" *Medical/Mrs.*, Vol. 1, No. 4, June 1978, p. 35.

96–98 "Dr. and Mrs. F. . . ." William H. Masters and Virginia E. Johnson. *Human Sexual Inadequacy*. Boston: Little Brown and Company, 1970, pp. 383–5.

101–102 "The most unfortunate . . ." Ibid., p. 87.

CHAPTER VI

105-106 "A problem peculiar . . ." Robert E. Taubman and
Harold I. Lief. "Doctors and Marriages: Their Special Pressures." *Medical World News*, February 7, 1977, p. 38.
106-109 "Physicians live in . . ." Judith Alter. "Doctors and
Dalliance: Fact or Fiction?" *Medicial/Mrs.*, Vol. 1, No. 6,
January 1979, p. 17.
110 "No wonder wives . . ." Shainberg. *Brain Surgeon*, p. 88.
111 "There aren't many . . ." Ibid.
112 "Statistically, the most . . ." Mark Holoweiko. "Extra Marital
Sex: Sometimes It Helps." *Medical Economics*, October 1,
1979, pp. 51-5. Copyright © 1979 by Litton Industries, Inc.
Published by Medical Economics Company, a Litton division,
at Oradell, N.J. 07649. Reprinted by permission.
114 "Medical Meetings: I Fear . . ." Anne Wang. *Medical/Mrs.*,
Vol. 1, No. 4, June 1978, p. 33.
115 "analysis of 57,514 . . ." K. Daniel Rose and Irving Rosow.
"Marital Stability Among Physicians." *California Medicine*,
Vol. 16, March 1972, p. 95.
117 "Indeed some doctors . . ." Holoweiko. *Medical Economics*,
p. 58.
121-122 "As a couple . . ." Ibid., p. 63.
126-127 "successful in demeaning . . ." Miles, Krell, and Lin.
"The Doctor's Wife . . ." *International Journal of Psychiatry in
Medicine*, April 1975, pp. 482-3.

CHAPTER VII

135 "discouragement regarding the . . ." Herbert C. Modlin and
Alberto Montes. "Narcotics Addiction in Physicians." *The
American Journal of Psychiatry*, Vol. 21, 1964, pp. 362-3.
Copyright © 1964, The American Psychiatric Association.
135 "adolescent fantasy . . ." Ibid.
135 "disillusionment and reactive . . ." Ibid.
137 "A Wisconsin gynecologist . . ." Giovanna Breu. "Medics."
People Weekly, September 24, 1979, p. 45.
138-141 "One of the basic . . ." John F. Halenar. "Drinking and
Drugs: Behind the Hard Numbers." *Medical Economics*, Octo-

ber 1, 1979, pp. 109–18. Copyright © 1979 by Litton Industries, Inc. Published by Medical Economics Company, a Litton Division, at Oradell, N.J. 07649. Reprinted by permission.

144–145 "SAFER: How long . . ." "Doctor, Are You Hooked?" CBS 60 *Minutes*, December 10, 1978. Copyright © 1978, CBS, Inc.

146 "In August 1974 . . ." LeClair Bissell and Al J. Mooney. "The Special Problem of the Alcoholic Physician." *Medical Times*, June 1975, p. 63.

147 "Only three of . . ." Modlin and Montes. "Narcotics Addiction in Physicians." *The American Journal of Psychiatry*, Vol. 21, 1964, p. 361. Copyright © 1964, The American Psychiatric Association.

151 "The Doctor and His Marriage." Jerry M. Lewis. *Texas Medicine*, Vol. 61, August 1965, p. 615.

151 "Psychiatric Illness in the Physician's Wife." Evans. *American Journal of Psychiatry*, August 1965, p. 160.

CHAPTER VIII

154 "believes that the enjoyment . . ." Marguerite Hurrey Wolf. *How to Be a Doctor's Wife Without Really Dying*. Sarasota: Booklore Publishers, 1978.

154–155 "What the doctor's . . ." Ibid., p. 80.

155 "Whereas she used to be . . ." Ibid.

155 "Doctors' wives more . . ." Harold Marcus. "What Causes Those Medical School Marriages to Falter?" *Medical/Mrs.*, Vol. 1, No. 4, July 1978, p. 35.

157 "negotiated beforehand . . ." Kathleen T. Jordan. "The Unhappy Doctor's Spouse—Myth or Reality?" *Facets*, Vol. 40, No. 3, Summer 1979, p. 4.

157 "spirited defense of . . ." Denis L. Breo. "Phil Donahue Show Gets Spirited Defense of Medical Marriages." *Facets*, Vol. 40, No. 3, Summer 1979, p. 5.

158 "It is only . . ." Peter J. Hampton. "The Doctor's Image." Unpublished article, 1980.

159 "meant to be . . ." Dennis L. Breo. "Man Bites Dog: One Happy Doctor's Wife." *Facets*, Vol. 40, No. 3, Summer 1979, p. 23.

159 "committed to help . . ." Ibid.
162–164 "Smile, You're the Doctor's Wife." Georgene Simon Dreishpoon. *Medical/Mrs.*, Vol. 1, No. 2, January/February 1978, p. 26.
165–166 "The Transformation." Rose-Ellen Benkel. *Medical/ Mrs.*, Vol. 1, No. 4, June 1978, p. 46.
166–167 "Yesterday I walked . . ." Cynthia S. Smith. "And What Do YOU Do?" *Medical/Mrs.*, Vol. 1, No. 6, January 1979, p. 5.
170 "I was the victim . . ." Bonnie Sashin. "Women Who Work: Declarations of Independence." *Medical/Mrs.*, Vol. 3, No. 1, March/April 1980, pp. 16–17.
172–173 "He has to . . ." Lawrence Hatterer. "Second Opinion." *Medical/Mrs.*, Vol. 1, No. 5, September/October 1978, p. 18.
175–178 "Why Should His Career Overshadow Mine?" Liz Hancock. *Medical/Mrs.*, Vol. 3, No. 1, March/April 1980, p. 44.
178–180 "Men forge ahead . . ." Cynthia S. Smith. "Women Who Work: Declarations of Independence." *Medical/Mrs.*, Vol. 1, No. 4, June 1978, p. 39.

CHAPTER IX

182 "When you join . . ." Phyllis Sinrich. "The Role of the Doctor's Wife." *Medical/Mrs.*, Vol. 1, No. 5, September/ October 1978, p. 16.
183–184 "A large number . . ." Copyright © 1966 by Martin L. Gross. *The Doctors.* New York: Random House, p. 318.
184 "Dr. James A. Halstead . . ." Ibid., p. 319.
184 "No demonstration is needed . . ." Ibid., p. 318.
185 "a man of mediocre . . ." Ibid., p. 324.
186–189 "Facing the Fee Factor . . ." Brenda Diaz. *Medical/ Mrs.*, Vol. 1, No. 4, June 1978, p. 42.
189–191 "Random Rules for Doctor-Wifing . . ." Marguerette Hosbach. *Medical/Mrs.*, Vol. 1, No. 6, January 1979, p. 18.
191 "In New York in 1960 . . ." Howard and Martha Lewis. *The Medical Offenders.* New York: Simon and Schuster, 1970.
193–194 "The AMA itself . . ." Gross. *The Doctors*, p. 536.
194 "I do not believe . . ." Ibid., p. 535
195–196 "Each day be . . ." Hosbach. "Random Rules . . ." *Medical/Mrs.*, January 1979, p. 18.

196–197   "We've had a couple . . ." Sinrich. "The Role." *Medical/ Mrs.*, September/October 1978, p. 17.

197–200   "When I or members . . ." Myra and Lawrence Hatterer. "Second Opinion." *Medical/Mrs.*, Vol. 1, No. 2, January/ February 1978.

200–201   "Our children learned . . ." Wolf. *How to Be a Doctor's Wife Without Really Dying*, pp. 74–8.

CHAPTER X

205–206   "Will the Real Doctor's Wife Stand Up?" Marie Gorman. *Granite: The New Hampshire Medical Society Auxiliary Bulletin*, Vol. XXVII, No. 1, Fall 1977, p. 2.

207–208   "But what of the needs . . ." Martha R. Fowlkes. *Behind Every Successful Man*. New York: Columbia University Press, 1980, pp. 185–6. Reprinted by permission.

Recommended Reading

Coombs, Robert H., and St. John, Joanne. *Making It in Medical School*. New York: Spectrum Publications, 1979.

Fowlkes, Martha R. *Behind Every Successful Man*. New York: Columbia University Press, 1980.

Glasser, Morton, and Pelto, Gretel. *The Medical Merry-Go-Round*. Pleasantville, N.Y.: Redgrave Publishing Co., 1980.

Gross, Martin L. *The Doctors*. New York: Random House, 1966.

Levinson, Daniel J. *The Seasons of a Man's Life*. New York: Alfred A. Knopf, 1978.

Lewis, Howard and Martha. *The Medical Offenders*. New York: Simon & Schuster, 1970.

Medical/Mrs. Kirby Lane, Rye, New York 10580.

Shainberg, Lawrence. *Brain Surgeon*. Philadelphia: Lippincott, 1979.

Wolf, Marguerite Hurrey. *How to Be a Doctor's Wife Without Really Dying*. Sarasota, N.Y.: Booklore Publishers, 1978.